AF479968

LOCKDOWN

**Defying a Global Pandemic
Through Travel and Adventure**

Table of Contents

Acknowledgements

 With any great project, there is always a long list of those who work tirelessly to help successfully complete the project. This book is the sum of hard work and support of many whom I wish to thank.

- To my daughters, who continuously encourage me to challenge myself with my adventures and my writing

- To Roberta Allison, for her wonderful "Forward" to this book, and for allowing my words to inspire her students

- To G.A. Hughes, Digital Design for producing my book, and creating the amazing cover concept

- To Wild Goose Escape Rooms for providing me the setting for the cover design

- To all of my family & friends who have supported the work that I do, who have followed along with many of my adventures, and continuously remind me to always go big

- To my beautiful grand daughter ***Tatum Ariyah Patterson***, to whom this book is dedicated to, because she provides me with a never-ending adventure.

Forward

Everybody loves a story. A story can teach, inspire, and entertain. Stories will take us to places we only dream of going. Paul Foster knows how to weave a story. This is why I choose Paul's last book, _On Top of the World_, as required reading for my students in an "Introduction to Tourism" class at a small community college in Wellesley, Massachusetts. I hoped what the students would take away from reading Paul's words would be a desire to explore other cultures. I also hoped they would take Paul's sage advice to seek a career they would be passionate about, and not to focus just on dollars.

Like his previous book, Paul's new book will transport readers to countries where they will learn what adventures await them and will also understand how different and yet how similar the people in other countries are to each other.

Writing _Lockdown_ during the pandemic inspired Paul to challenge his readers to reject the word "no" for an answer and to fight for one's dreams. Paul teaches us the therapeutic qualities of travel and how our trips will help us grow into the best version of ourselves.

We may not travel to every destination Paul takes us to in this book, but we certainly will enjoy some great stores along the journey.

Roberta Allison
Associate Professor, Hospitality Management

Introduction

"It was the best of times, it was the worst of times", it was the most insane of times. I don't think that last part is found in the famous beginning of the 1859 Charles Dickens classic *"A Tale of Two Cities"*. That most definitely was not the sentiment during the time his book was written, but if we fast forward 160 years to 2020, I can't think of a more appropriate definition to describe this 21st century year than insane. The major world events that have taken place during these last 2+ years, will surely have an entire piece of history devoted all to its own. A time when events forced the world to stop on a dime, and forever shift the paradigm of what we would consider to be normal.

Was it anything unique about what started in 2020, or was it just a cataclysmic chain of events that found the world in such disarray, at each other's throats, and hardening our mindsets to the point of "I am right, and you are wrong"? The truth is, I think many of the issues that came to the surface, had been bubbling for the previous two decades, and it took one very unexpected fuse to light the entire powder keg that would become 2020. Those chain of events started a period, that was at first so filled with promise, into something that would challenge my own sense of survival, and force me to challenge the establishment, and many friends, as each of us faced a new definition of self-preservation.

It is hard to imagine that a single year could shift so suddenly, from what had started out to be the foundation of what I thought would be my most adventurous year. A year that saw me look high into the sky on New Year's Eve 2019, amid a -8-degree evening to watch in awe as the Aurora Borealis (Northern Lights) danced in the nighttime Alaskan sky. A trip that saw me celebrate New Year's Day crossing the Arctic Circle, something that less than 1% of travelers to Alaska actually do. A trip that saw me achieve a couple of new firsts with a dog sled mushing ride, and swimming on a -20-degree day in an outdoor lake. With so much promise in the air, and me really following an adventure travel concept that I have embraced for the last several years, the second decade of the millennium was truly going to be greater than great. How quickly and dramatically things changed, and how 2020, started a new paradigm that may be remembered as a monumental place in time for all of the wrong reasons.

Lockdown, is a snap shot of time, through my eyes particularly, but with an emphasis on the overall perspective of society, and my reaction to do it. Each chapter will highlight an important period of what we would soon call "pandemic", and how that event affected me, and quite possibly you. As I mentioned in my previous book "On Top of The World", the concept of an adventure is not limited to traveling around the world or country, but any item that has had a profound effect on your life. As you read, you will discover that the pandemic period offered very little travel for most people in the traditional sense, and yet, I took those events and made them adventures in my own eyes. I challenged the traditional narrative by continuing to have some adventure travels, and refused to live a life of fear. The fact that I did not travel particularly for business anywhere close to what I normally do, was an adventure in itself.

Some of the topics will offer strong opinions that you may agree with, or strongly disagree with, and perhaps you might even find offensive. As the world today has increasingly found more things that are offensive than are not, I am sure that my take on things is likely to offend someone. We are living in a time when now more than ever, simple respect for someone's opinion is a rare commodity. My goal, for you the reader, is to hear from my perspective these events, and how given the environment that I currently live, leave you recognizing that we may all be in the same storm, but we are not all in the same boat. For anyone who may find some of my perspective's offensive, let us agree on one aspect, there are no refunds!

Enjoy the timeline in review.

1.

The Enemy Within

It started out as a typical Friday morning in early January with a traditional Southern California Winter temperature of about 70 degrees. I must say after 33 years of living here, I have become quite used to the mild Winters, and today was no different. Having just returned from my Arctic Alaskan Adventure, I was no doubt ready for some pleasant weather after experiencing a -28 temperature upon my departure from Fairbanks. Still feeling the physical effects of my recent trip, I had a relatively light work day scheduled, and even a bit of fun, as I had a meeting with some local rental car vendors to discuss a mutual client. There was no indication that anything out of the ordinary was about to happen, but as I took my first bite of a turkey club sandwich complements of the **Yard House**, that would soon change.

It was somewhere after that first bite during our lunch meeting that my text message buzzer went off, and sent me into a posture that I would not soon forget. It was at this time that my friend Christine had sent me a text, with a link to a news article announcing that **Neil Peart**, drummer & lyricist for the band **Rush**, and someone that I have idolized since I was 12 years old, had died of brain cancer. The shock that flowed through me right then and there was indescribable, so much so that I could not finish my lunch, and our meeting ended early. I immediately needed to return home so that I could verify the authenticity of this news, as we are all aware that many hoax type stories permeate the Internet. Sadly, the news was true, and indeed a very important figure within my life was suddenly gone.

Now my reaction to this news may seem a bit extreme and not a real adventure to the average person, but this was not an ordinary situation within my life, but a profound change that you just think will never happen per se. I have lived within the Hollywood cesspool of celebrities for over 33 years, and in past writings, I have been very vocal of my disdain for the whole celebrity crowd, and have advocated the notion that they are no more important, than any one of us. I have also been very critical of those in the elite world who try to use their fame as a mechanism to manipulate others, and guide their point of view, particularly as it pertains to politics. I have been even more critical of everyday people who allow themselves to be guided by another's views, simply because that person is famous. I will actually touch more upon that in a later chapter to avoid going off on a tangent here. So, what was it about the passing of Neil Peart that affected me so much, and why did this man transcend my usual loathing of the "famous" crowd, and have such an impact on my life? In order to better understand that question, we have to go back 46 years in time to where it all began.

It was the Summer of 1974, and as a budding 10-year-old, I had the benefit of a brother 5 years my senior. He came home with a new album by a band called Rush, and proceeded to play it day and night, until I had no choice but to accept the tunes as part of my day. But it wasn't until about 3 years later when things started to change for me. This time, he came home with a new "Live" Rush album, and while I recognized some of the songs, there was something new about the music. I would later find out that the original drummer for the band, had left the group after the first album, and the drummer on this "live" album was a guy named Neil Peart. I was well entrenched in my own drumming by this time, but listening to this guy, things changed rapidly for me. For those who follow music, drummers for the most part are considered part of the rhythm section of a band. The guitarist will solo every song, and the singer will move about with stage presence, but drummers are designed to keep the beat. That was until Neil Peart came on the scene, and as **Taylor Hawkins (RIP) of the Foo Fighters** so eloquently stated in a Hall of Fame Induction speech in 2013, *"brought the drums to the fucking forefront"*. It was then I realized that I had discovered the person who would establish my musical high bar, but I had no idea how much that bar would be continually raised.

As a drummer myself, Neil established the standard that I would hold myself to, as I continued to work on my own skills. The ultimate in achievement was to be able to play a Rush song, with some semblance of cohesiveness. I knew I wasn't skilled enough to play all the parts, but I would always challenge myself to try. It was during these formidable years in the 1980's that I started to feel connected to this individual in other ways than just drumming. Neil Peart was an amazing lyricist for the band, and as they started to grow in popularity, he started writing more and more about the trappings of being in the public eye, and just how uncomfortable he was with the concept of fame. A feeling that I often had, not from a fame standpoint, because I wasn't famous, but just the notion of people who view you differently because you happen to have a certain gift and ability. I always felt I was the same person, I was just able to do something that not a lot of other people could do, and it made me uncomfortable. There were many themes in his lyrics that I could relate to, and as I grew in age, I started to understand the cerebral meanings of what he was saying in his songs.

The one constant in my life during these years was music, and it was no accident that when cataclysmic events took place, like my first high school break up, I could rely on the challenges of playing "***Tom Sawyer***", to get me through the moments. I had the opportunity to see Neil play live in every decade from the 70,'s through the last show I saw in 2007. That show was sort of a passing of the torch for me, because I was now a parent, taking my daughter to her first Rush concert. Watching my daughter Katie enjoy music that I listened to when I was her age, was such a surreal feeling for me. While she did not gravitate to the level of air drumming that I did, she nonetheless understood a true master at his profession. The most magnificent thing about watching and listening to Neil play live, was that every song was played live exactly as it sounded on the studio album. I was always amazed at how through all those years, the songs were still played precisely as when they were first recorded, in some cases 30 or more years before.

By the time the 1990's rolled in, things had changed in my life, and I was unable to be as a devoted fan as I had been for many years before. Marriage and family started to take hold, and while I still listened to the music, the everyday goings on with the band, had taken somewhat of a backseat in my life. It was during these years that Neil experienced personal tragedy with the passing of his daughter, and wife within a span of 10 months. Because of those events, the band took a hiatus, and no one really knew if we would ever hear from Neil Peart again. Certainly, he had made his mark on the music industry already, and no one would have begrudged him if he had decided to call it a career. It was during this time that he would branch out into new areas, that would later become another connection point for me. Being an accomplished lyricist, it seemed only natural that he would string many of those themes together and start to write books. Neil Peart became an accomplished author, and his book *"Ghost Rider"* chronicles his return from personal tragedy to once again play music. It was here that I discovered my own love of writing, and provided the motivation that I needed to publish my own books. I have 4 of Neil's books in my library, and each tells a story about life, and how we are only here for a short period of time.

Once the new millennium kicked in, and my kids started their formidable years, there was time to devote to my own music, and those who I had listened to. I got back into drumming again, as I got a set of *Tama* drums as a Christmas present, and proceeded to pick up where I had left off some 10 years earlier. Though a bit rusty in some areas, I was pleased at how much I had retained, and yes, I went right back to testing myself against the gold standard, new Rush material. During this period in my life, I became a heavy reader, and some of that material included books written by Neil Peart. In 2007, during the Snakes & Arrows tour that visited Irvine, CA, I got to finally share the music of Rush with my daughter. I was in essence introducing my daughter to something that held so much meaning in my life for more than 35 years. I also remember that many of the lyrics on that album, were paralleling my life, with much change and upheaval. I often found myself living the actual lyrics to the song *"Far Cry"*, from the Snakes & Arrows album, as I entered a lengthy period of uncertainty.

For as long as there is music, there will also be debate, especially when it comes to defending your idols as some of the best in the business. All musicians have their own personal inspirations, and mine can't really be a mystery here, as I have donated the first chapter of this book, to a man who inspired and motivated me. It is this sort of adulation that made Neil so uncomfortable about his abilities, and possibly where the masses ranked him on the list of top drummers. But when a musician at the top of his game, decides that he has lost some of that greatness, and decides to start taking drum lessons 20 years after turning professional. That is the true sign on the consummate professional, and why he has always been ranked within the top 5 of drummers, based on many different poles.

By the time the Rush 40th Anniversary tour rolled around in 2014, there had been much talk that the tour would be the final live performances for the band. We all know that at some point bands will eventually call it a career. Some unfortunately wait way too long before they call it a day, and often the lack of fans actually make that call for them. That was not the case with R40, at least from a competency perspective. Certainly, the band had achieved everything possible, with the crowning touch being a spot in the Rock N Roll Hall of Fame in 2013. But still, the thought of no more Rush music, and no more Neil Peart drumming was a sobering thought. Sure enough, as the tour ended, the retirement talk persisted, and was made even more concrete when Neil did an interview that stated he was officially a retired drummer. No one really knew the finality of that statement, possibly even the man himself as we would find out in January 2020.

Neil Peart passed away on January 7th, 2020 at the age of 67. His death was formally announcement on January 10th. To say the music world was shocked would be a gross understatement, and I would be so bold as to say the whole world was shocked. The cause, as with so many others was cancer. Brain cancer to be more precise. The fact that most of the world knew nothing of his battle is not a surprise. This was a very private man, who despised fame, and all that came with it. A man who deep down inside had to know that his skills as a drummer, and lyricist, were second to none, yet would never think of himself in that way. A man whose greatest achievement by his own words was to inspire others to pursue their dreams. Yet, it was the very title of this chapter that had the final say as ***the enemy within***, managed to claim another person before their time.

After I heard about his death, the loss I felt during this period of time was significant, and indeed I took time to reflect on my memories and places in time where I was truly inspired by an individual I had never met. My own personal Social Media tribute post was met with some unexpected comfort, as many longtime friends offered their thoughts into this man's influence in my life.

- **Don Hamm:** "As soon as I heard about his passing I thought of you. Very sad"
- **Tim Bofo:** "I thought of you as soon as I saw this. I remember you idolized this guy in high school."
- **Don Wise:** "Sorry to hear that Paul, I know what an influence he was on your drumming, simply brilliant !!!!!

While Neil may not have been comfortable with the accolades that poured in from so many diverse places, I took a sense of pride knowing that the world had finally stood up and took notice of the **Professor**. Yes, there were the traditional headlines from standard music bearer **Rolling Stone** and the like, but check out these headlines from the far corners of journalism:

- Why has Neil Peart's death affected so many?
- The Misfit Awesomeness of Neil Peart and Rush
- Rush's Neil Peart left behind a lyrical legacy
- Remembering Neil Peart, A Monster Drummer with A Poet's Heart

When NPR, and the New York Times take time out of their busy political agendas to write about you, you must have made an impact along the way. For my final thoughts on his passing, I can only say that he guided me, inspired me, challenged me, and saved me in ways that no one but myself will ever truly know. The most important thing is that his music and words will continue to do all of those things, long after his physical being is gone. I think the final lyric inspiration I will include sums up the life of Neil Peart, and though I will forever have an unfulfilled bucket list item, a piece of him has lived inside me for many years.

2.

It's the End of The World as We Know It
(And I Feel Fine)

Kind of an ominous title to this chapter, but one that seems appropriate for what was going to happen not only to me, but the world at large. That might be a stretch, and certainly as February 2020 rolled in, there was no indication that anything out of the ordinary was at play. Yes, I took my 30-day mourning of Neil Peart and parlayed that into a musical Rush dedication on the iPhone, but my take was simply, we had our "bad" moment early in the year, so it's out of the way. Now it was time to get serious, and map out the adventure strategy for 2020, and what an adventure it was going to be. For the last several years, I had toyed with the idea of going to Africa. It was a continent that I had never been to, so it was still a bucket list item. Several factors played into my previous decisions to by-pass a trip there in favor of China and Russia, but my excuses and reasons ran aground, and now was the time. So, I mapped out a strategy that would have me heading to Egypt, Jordan and Israel in an attempt to experience my first pilgrimage. I will focus on that trip more in a coming chapter, but the planning stages were well underway by the end of January.

So, having my big international adventure mapped out in theory at least, I also wanted to check off a couple more local adventures that had been gnawing at me as well. Montana was still part of the elusive 3M's as I call them. There are 3 states that I have not visited in the US, Montana, Maine & Mississippi. It was now time to remove Montana from that list, so on a projected business trip to Headquarters in Salt Lake City in April, it seemed like the time to take a couple of extra days, and head to ***Yellowstone National Park.*** The month of April was perfect because the weather most likely would not be a factor, and the crowd element would be favorable as well. Another first would be Mt. Rushmore in South Dakota, as I had a Denver conference planned in July, and the drive over was only 4 hours. I could throw in a bit of hiking in Custer National Park, and check one more item off that bucket list. Everything was lining up perfectly, and then March 12th fell on the calendar, and not since September 11th, 2001 has a date meant so much to so many.

13

For the previous couple of months, the "Maim" Stream Media (Yes,
I spelled it correctly), had been spouting on about the latest in what
had become an election year virus story. The world has had numerous
other virus scares most notably since the millennium, SARS, Bird Flu,
E.coli, Ebola to name a few, and the origin of these viruses in many cases
seemed to be the country of China. This however was different, because
it was reasoned that a pandemic could be weaponized into a political
tool, and thus Corona Virus or Covid-19, as it was officially ushered into to
everyone's vocabulary.

The Controversy Begins

I think it is important to remove all the elephants in the room before we
proceed any further. 1. The thoughts expressed in this chapter are my
own opinions, and no one else's. 2. They may or may not agree with
your thoughts, but that does not make them any less right or wrong, and
only further illustrates the concept that I talked about in previous books
of ***"where you stand, depends on where you sit"***. 3. For every article of
"fact" that you can produce that supports your belief, I can provide the
same many "facts" that support mine. Finally, 4. I am considered "High
Risk" from a medical perspective regarding this Pandemic, so I do have
a vested interest, and role to play. Having outlined the elephants, let's
take a look at what transpired, and how society will never be the same
because of it.

I happened to be traveling to Salt Lake City for a customer meeting on
March 12th. That was also the day that President Trump announced
that pretty much the entire country would be shut down from arriving
aircraft from international destinations, mainly from Europe at the time.
A travel ban from China had actually been implemented several weeks
earlier, but this was different because it was coming from the Western
World, and not what many considered the source of the virus. Once that
ban was announced, the travel industry did an absolute nose dive, as
almost immediately customers stopped all their travelers from traveling.
The next day, the local school districts got into panic mode, and effective
immediately canceled all classes for what was initially thought to be a
2-week period. For the schools to take such a drastic measure there must
have been a good reason, and for the most part, most people were on

board with the precautions, because let's face it, this was new, and we just didn't know enough about any of this.

Things were literally changing by the hour, and that gave the world's number one nemesis (The Media) a chance to capitalize on yet another entertainment opportunity. My disdain for Main Stream Media is not a secret, as I feel it serves no purpose other than to sensationalize usually tragic or crisis events, in an effort to win entertainment points. If you are one that still feels that media news has as its first priority the goal to inform the public, you might want to check and see who pays the bills. Media news, like many other industries, is run by corporate sponsors, and those sponsors demand viewers. If your viewership is not there, the sponsors will dry up as well. After having several years of promoting failed investigations, and election tampering claims that amounted to nothing more than tax payer wasted dollars, they needed a big win, and boy did they get it by creating panic. Stories of the new global threat Covid-19 virus were running 24/7, and sadly this actually did create panic among consumers, who based on recommendations from media, began buying up certain goods in mass amounts. This created shortages of items such as hand sanitizer, facial tissues, and most notably toilet paper. As people were now buying 50 or more rolls of toilet paper, the stores could not keep them in stock. Stories of people fighting over toilet paper in stores became the norm, and the media was only too happy to show us the footage of a desperate society out of control, and fighting for their share of toilet paper and Top Ramen.

All of this panic buying led to stores having to change operational procedures, as they were closing earlier to be able to re-stock the goods that were flying off the shelves. Special hours were established for Senior Citizens because it was discovered that they were not able to get necessary supplies as people continued to horde. While all of this panic buying was going on, State Governments were telling everyone to stay home, and forcing business that were deemed non-essential to close indefinitely, forcing millions of people out of work, and onto the unemployment line. Standard retail stores, dine in restaurants, places of worship, and even personal hygiene businesses were ordered closed, as they were labeled "non-essential". Exempt from all this were the big box retailers, grocery stores, and interestingly enough liquor stores, and of course Lottery centers. Those in charge deemed it was too dangerous for people to get a haircut, but standing in line at a Wal Mart or to buy lottery tickets was safe and essential. It was around this time that I started having my doubts as to what was really at play here. Most people probably don't pay close enough attention to recognize some of these essential elements that were allowed to remain in operation, are heavily regulated by government in the form of tax revenues. Alcohol in most states has huge amounts of what are known as "sin taxes", and to restrict their purchase means less money for government. The lottery is a pure form of legalized gambling that EVERY state offers. The proceeds from every ticket sold is a 100% profit for the State, as there is no middle man. Think about that, and ask yourself, is the lottery or liquor stores essential for humanity's survival, or governments?

It Hits Close to Home

All of this whirlwind was bound to affect everyone, and my family and I were no exception. Let's face it, I use toilet paper just like the rest of us, and I face the same dilemma as
you, if I run out. There were a couple trips I made specifically to secure my favorite 2-ply brand, only to be turned away as no-ply was available on the store shelves. The next strategy was to go to the unconventional places for the elusive "bathroom tissue", which had me show up at the "essential" Home Depot or Staples, but to no avail, as those shelves were void of the fluffy stuff as well. Things were getting serious, and the very real thought of paper towels taking on a new role (pun intended), had entered my mind. So yes, as crazy as it may sound, finding toilet paper actually became my first adventure of 2020. In the end, like so many other things in life, when one has strings, you must pull them. A call to my daughter's boyfriend who worked for a food service distributor, secured me a bulk box of 50 rolls, at a wholesale price. Upon delivery, I was so happy I sang a few bars of the Charmin song.

So, once I had secured my wiping future for the next several months at least, it was time to turn my attention to ensure that my family was safe, and fully understanding of what was real, and what was political pandemic. I have always prided myself on encouraging my daughters to be involved in the democratic process. I have never told them how to vote, or who to support because I believe it is their right and duty to draw their own conclusions. To educate themselves about how our system of government works, and determine if it works in the manner they would like it to. Unfortunately, the vast majority of American voters have no clue how are system of government works, or the mechanisms in place to ensure it works, or enact change if a majority of the people desire that change. Most people take their cues from media sound bites, and/or celebrities, whether they be entertainment or sports dedicated. What this time in our history would demonstrate is that, in a time when we should be researching the facts more than ever, most people were willing to accept what media, politicians, and political appointees told us were facts. Those who questioned or dug deeper into those facts were labeled "conspiracy theorists" or deniers of science. While I would not consider myself a denier of science, I am someone who insists we look at all the science, and not just cherry pick the parts that favor the popular narrative. Based on the science after many months of Covid cases, the only number that really mattered was that the mortality rate from this virus was less than 1%. If you are one that feels that is not an acceptable number, then you clearly have an issue with the fact that death is a part of life, and it will always be. No one can escape facing death whether it be someone close to you, or your own mortality, it is the one constant in life. We as a society better get a handle on that notion, or we will allow that fear to control everything we do.

Being in the minority of people who refused to panic, there were some close to me who questioned why I did not take all of this seriously, and why I was adamant about continuing to live my life the way I had done for so many years prior to all of this. As I mentioned at the top of this chapter, I am considered to be a person in a high-risk category. In 2009 I was diagnosed with Psoriatic Arthritis, which is an autoimmune disorder. Prior to this diagnosis, I battled psoriasis plaques that would appear on my skin in a variety of areas like my back, or elbows, even sometimes on my legs. In addition to that, the condition also caused a significant amount of inflammation in extremity joints like fingers, ankles, and sometimes my shoulders. At 45 years old I often would wake up and feel perhaps I was 65, as it would sometimes take 30 minutes to work the stiffness loose in the morning.
I have been blessed to be able to take a medication that alleviates not

only the psoriasis part of this disorder, but the arthritis piece as well. When the doctor first told me about the medication, he explained exactly what it was, and the risks in taking what is commonly termed an Immune suppressant. The two big factors were an increase in likelihood of infections, and yes, an increase in the possibility of cancer. The C Word!! He also told me that I would have to be careful of certain things, to take some new precautions, and if I were to get sick, to get into to seek treatment right away, and not wait a few days to see how things would go. I was fully informed of all the potential risks, and how I would have to live my life moving forward if I wanted to have relief from what was causing me to slow down, and be in considerable discomfort. I did not hesitate a second about trying this medication, because what I did not want was to be limited in how I lived my active life. So, for the rest of my life, I knew I would need to take an injection once a week, and for me, that was a very small price to pay to be able to remain active. I want to stress that the medication I take is not lifesaving in the clinical sense, in that I do not need to take Enbrel in order to remain alive. However, from my perspective, living in pain, unable to move freely, and being relatively immobile is not living, it is existing, and I will never settle for that.

With all of this in mind, let me say that washing my hands, and being cautious around others who may be sick is not a new phenomenon to me. I have been washing my hands long before March 2020 when Dr. Fauci told everyone this was the latest trend. I've spent the last 35 years traveling around the world, flying in small cylinders, sitting next to thousands of people, never once making a fashion statement by wearing a mask. I have been to some of the most unsanitary places in the world, and have visited the notorious "wet markets" in China, never eating myself, but watching locals eat. Through all of this I have never once had an issue, but now I am being asked to throw out all of that actual experience, because a government agency announces be afraid, be very afraid. Something that drastic and that unprecedented requires I ask questions. If you are willing to believe that someone else is looking out for you, then you are openly ignoring the entire evolution of man, which up to this point, has consistently preyed upon itself to further its self-interest.

None of the points that I am raising here is going to garner me an invitation to the next CDC event, or briefing, nor can they disprove any of what I am saying, because they simply don't know. My contention all along is that they are not being honest with people, and omitting certain truths for political reasons. Remember when the early slogan was that "flatten the curve" garbage, and they said everyone had to do their part in order to "stop the spread" of the virus? Then when the supposed curve got flattened, we had to now wait until there was a vaccine. Have you noticed "stop the spread" is no longer in the vernacular having been replaced by "slow the spread"? That is because the virus is never going away, the same way all other viruses never go away, the simply become irrelevant because of the body's immune system. Yes, there are vaccines that have helped create the antibodies that one has to fight off these viruses, but they never go away. I often hear people rumble on about once the virus goes away, or if people would only wear masks, then the virus would be gone. That isn't going to happen, but there are people who want you to believe that's true, so that you will accept their every word, and not research for yourself. I would also like to say that I am in no way anti-vaccine, nor am I at the point of thinking about micro chips etc. I have received many vaccinations as a child, and even as an adult. I get my annual flue shot because my doctor recommends, and sometimes it works, and sometimes it doesn't as I get the flue occasionally, just like the rest of us. What I am, is anti-panic and fear, and creating an atmosphere where people are so scared to leave their homes because they are afraid that will catch a virus, by walking past another person on the street.

The Questions I Ask

So, by now you might be asking why I feel this way? What has made me so cynical that I would question the very institutions that have sworn to protect us? The short answer is my experience, and my understanding of the political process. Having spent years of studying politics in the form of two college degrees, working public sector positions, and following the political process since I was a teenager, I have pause about how the process has been corrupted over time, and how it will always have an end game of the haves and have nots.

Specifically, as it relates to the virus, one of the biggest questions I have had is why there is no government push to improve one's individual health. Since I do not want to be a science denier, I think we can all agree that strengthening our immune system would certainly be an asset in fighting any virus infection. Yet there has been no propaganda campaign to encourage people to make healthier decisions, exercise more, strengthen their immune system by eating better, or improving their mental health. Each time the virus cases supposedly spiked, the government response was to close gyms, and other health driven businesses as a means to slow the spread.

What you did see were propaganda campaigns telling people to stay home, watch TV, and by all means order fast food for delivery. Using buzz words and phrases alike "Alone Together" or the ever popular "Stay Home, Save Lives". Why would you not encourage people to take better care of themselves, and put them in the best position to fight any infection that comes their way? Why would you not encourage your citizenry to enact behaviors that represent a Duane Johnson rather than a Michael Moore? Unless your goal is to create a completely dependent society, that is incapable of taking care of, or thinking for themselves to the point that basic survival is dependent upon someone else.

It was because of this question, and others of course that I chose to take my health and my life into my own hands. I was not going to buy into all the hysteria and fear that the media was peddling, nor would I for a second take the word of politicians. A fair question to ask could be "who am I to question the motives of the media or politicians". But as I mentioned earlier regarding my academic background, having written numerous term papers on the subject of political power, and even worked for government agencies in previous roles, I consider myself someone who has enough experience and information to form an educated opinion, with no ulterior motive other than seeking the truth.

So just who could I trust, or be willing to entertain as a legitimate source for the real facts about the Corona Virus? Certainly, the medical field would be the first place to start, and indeed early on we were all wowed by Dr. Anthony Fauci, the head of the CDC. Fauci is considered to be the foremost expert in Immunology, so what could be the problem? I became skeptical of fraud Fauci because he was the head of a government agency, and the number one thing that a government agency wants more than anything else is funding! What better way to generate sympathy for increased funding than a pandemic. We have long in this country believed that we can throw money at a problem, and that will solve it. This strategy is continuously tried and continues to fail, particularly in the education sector where no matter how much funding is increased, our public-school system continues to lag behind other countries.

I started to become suspicious of the Fauci plan, when rather than dedicating his time to solving the crisis, he managed to find time to appear on prime-time cable news shows, and soon became the late-night rock star, and daytime cover of the major newspapers. The funny thing about becoming a celebrity is that there always seems to be someone watching or listening to every word you say. That became apparent when initially Fauci was telling everyone that the use of masks had no benefit, then he flipped on that a month later and muddied the water more. It was important to wear masks even outdoors until a picture of him along with other family members was taken at a Washington Nationals baseball game with his life saving mask lowered below his chin. Speaking from a political perspective, the "optics" of that photo was not a good look for him, and only served to question his real motives even more. For me, I will simply wait for his tell-all book that I'm sure is coming in the future.

Whether or not you feel the questions I raise hold any merit, or if there is even a foundation to have any questions, can be debated. What cannot be disputed is that the country is divided as to what the real facts of the whole virus situation are, and that the political implications of it are intertwined. While it may not be the end of the world as we know it, there are a lot of people who feel that way.

3.

That's What Friends Are For

The element of friendship is as old as man itself, and holds such an important role in our existence that it would be impossible for the concept of friendship not to be affected by what 2020 was dishing out. Traditional friends come and go for most people throughout our lives, and with the exception of the few really lifelong friends that we will have, any given person could have possibly 100 or so people that they would consider friends over a lifetime. It's because of elements that happen within our lives that these basic friendships often come and go. Up until 2020, I am hard pressed to think of any topic that places a true challenge to the concept of friendship more than politics.

Politics, and a loss or distancing from friends is certainly not a new concept, but I do believe it has become much more galvanized over the course of the last 20 years. Occasionally when there is an event that effects a vast majority of people, political discourse sometimes finds itself taking a backseat for a greater united front. The 9/11 attacks on America is an example of where everyone seemed to come together, and stand united if only for a brief period in time. During that time, we stood as one against an identifiable enemy, in this case, Radical Extremism. It didn't take long for the kumbaya moments to fade, and probably by the holiday season, everyone was back to arguing politics over the Thanksgiving turkey.

Given that example, and similar trends over a significant historical period, one might think that the first identified pandemic in over 100 years would be enough to stop the political sniping, in favor of a more "we're all in this together" attitude. However, 2020 ushered in a hybrid mentality where political discourse joined forces with a sudden wealth of medical knowledge amongst all Americans to form the biggest 2 headed monster of hate and contempt for fellow citizens, that honestly I can't remember ever existing in my lifetime. "Hate" is such a strong word, and one that I don't relish using, but if anyone just browsed a social media site on any given day, I'm not sure what other word could be used to describe the experience? Political differences, spirited debate, differences of opinion, please! Maybe if you included the words "on steroids" to any of those definitions, you could possibly make that case.

So how did we arrive at a point where a contagious virus that affected indiscriminately, without regard to any political affiliations whatsoever, take on the persona and characteristics of what we have all become accustomed to in our political lives? My answer is that those who control the political narratives (ON ALL SIDES), recognized that political gains could be made by weaponizing a health issue, in an attempt to further their political agenda. In order for this plan to succeed, you must galvanize the masses into your way of thinking, and let them do your bidding for you at the local levels, as well as cyberspace.

In the early days of the pandemic, back in March of 2020, so much was happening so fast that most of us were just trying to get a handle on what was happening. Schools were closing, stores were limiting the number of shoppers, and their open/close hours. There was no real time to take a particular position, as we simply didn't comprehend what was really occurring, and quite possibly we were still in denial that it was even happening. But once we had a couple of weeks in, and the media and politicians started telling us what to believe, we staked out our claim. It was right around this time that everyone graduated with their medical degrees from the prestigious Facebook School of Medicine, and decided to impart their new-found knowledge on the masses. Suddenly everyone was an expert in immunology, and if you thought differently, from someone else, you were quickly corrected.

The reality to this tongue-in-cheek analysis is that most people became nothing more than a parrot to what was being plastered all over the media air waves whether it be politicians or the "top" medical people in their field, as appointed by those said politicians. So, with tensions running high, it is not surprising that these feelings spilled over into friendships, and left a great deal of carnage in their wake. As a result, many friendships were lost, irreparably damaged, or just plain never the same, once the virus fear peaked beyond "it's a whole lot of nothing" stage. That is probably the one and only statement that everyone would probably agree with. But to what extent could this situation possibly go to? Well, for me it started in the family arena, and managed to touch all phases of friendship throughout the year.

So, let me start with the family element, because that is always the one that is closest to the heart for most people. We often make jokes about family gatherings during the holidays, and how they often end up being political debates with a little turkey and mashed potatoes tossed in. Now throw in the hysteria of a pandemic, and you have the makings of a serious case for a "Christmas with the Kranks" attitude for next year. Well in my case maybe it was "Summer with the Kranks", because I felt the scorn of expressing my opinion from extended family. You see, I dared to comment on a social media post where I questioned why the immortal Dr. Fauci seemed to be more interested in making the rounds on the late-night talk show circuit, rather than finding solutions to the problem he so adamantly stated was serious. To which a cousin of mine replied, and I must put this disclaimer out there. ***"Some may consider this vulgar, so if harsh language is something you find offensive, you may wish to move on"***. I would also like to say that I am not offended by these words, but I personally would never say them to anyone, though I probably would think them at times. I share this to demonstrate the depth of someone who would tell you they are tolerant and accepting of other's views. You be the judge of that statement.

"What a fucking ignorant, loser asshole you are Paul Foster. There I said it! Sorry Alyssa. Sorry Susan. Paul Foster, I've had enough of your Fox News- teat sucking, Breibart butt-f-g delusional nonsense. You've spent your loser life watching television and it shows! If you want to discuss further, you can call me. If you want to sulk, and think you deserve an apology, dream on."

I wonder what Vegas would have the odds at ***"Wanting to discuss further"***? I was surprised by the response, but not completely shocked. You see if 2020 has communicated anything so clearly, it is that those who claim to be the most tolerant, are anything but. For my own sake, I lost no sleep, received immediate family support, and saved the postage of one Christmas card, so all is well. I did have to employ the dreaded "Facebook Block", as a few more English Vocabulary lessons found their way on to my "timeline" soon after that post. Truth be told, the biggest affront to me was that she spelled my daughter's name incorrectly. I won't glorify this section any longer other than to say, that family no longer appears to be off limits when it comes to politics.

This wasn't the only difference in family when it comes to current affairs. I have 3 daughters, and each of them are their own person. I don't expect, nor do I require my daughters to share the same views as me, but I do require them to respect that everyone has a different perspective, and as long as that perspective remains peaceful and respectful, they need to extend the same courtesy. My daughters have their own views, and rather than highlight the differences, I celebrate their participation in the process. I have encouraged each of them to research the issues, and draw their own conclusions. The election of 2020 saw my youngest daughter **Megan** exercise her right to vote for the first time, and I honor that regardless of whatever her views are. What I have taught them is the right to let their voice be heard through the vote, is the very foundation our country was founded upon. Yes, in today's world that is skeptical, but the principle itself remains valid.

Friends with Benefits

Another element of friendship that was thrust into a negative spotlight because of Covid was work colleagues. As the floor of the travel industry pretty much disintegrated in a matter of days around the "ides of March", my company, like almost every other company was forced to make tough personnel decisions. For the first time in the company's 30-year history, employee layoffs became a reality. The travel industry in general has gone through many upheavals throughout the 35 years I have been associated with it. Surging fuel prices, global political unrest, economic recession, commission cuts, and of course 9/11, all have been storms that the travel and tourism industry has been asked to bear over the past couple of decades. Each time, the industry has been able to weather the storm, and realize continued growth. Given the past history, there was reason to believe that Covid-19 was just another storm that needed to be weathered, and we would soon be back on track as had been the case so many times before.

As the layoff announcements were made, there were two overwhelming thoughts going through my mind. The first one was "not again", as I had just re-emerged from the ashes of being laid off in 2018, where it took me over 10 months to find a new permanent position that I am at now. The physical and mental challenges that experience presented me with, were so profound that I needed to seek professional counseling to combat the depression, self-loathing, and feelings of utter failure that overwhelmed me on a daily basis. I simply would not be strong enough to have to go through this again, and at a time where millions of other people were in the same boat.

The second aspect that entered my mind at that moment was that people that I worked with, many had become new found friends as I celebrated my first-year anniversary with the company, would be laid off. People being laid off from their jobs is pretty much an everyday thing in today's world, but when it is someone that is close to you, it takes on a whole different persona. Adding to this level of stress was the fact that many people who were laid off or furloughed, had more seniority with the company than I did. The level of survival guilt I felt those first couple of days after the fact, really took their toll on my overall feelings. As someone who was so freshly reminded of being in that situation, I had total empathy for those who were affected. Also hard to accept was that I quite possibly would no longer be working with them in the same capacity, and this after they helped me transition into my new role just one year before.

But I needed to carry on, even with a somewhat heavy heart. While I was grateful that I managed to stay among the ranks of employed, I also knew that I was going to have to take on a greater workload, as were other colleagues who remained with the company. Still, while all this was going on, it was always with the premise that this was a short-term situation, and after probably 90 days, this would all be over, and we would be back to regular staff, and regular customer travels like nothing had ever happened. Things became much gloomier as the Covid lion days of March, dragged on through the dog days of August. Each time there appeared to be favorable news that a corner had been turned, there were political reminders that the travel industry would not be returning to normal anytime soon. As of this writing, almost 11 months after the start of the 90 day slow down, things are very slowly starting to improve.

It is estimated that it could take several years for my industry to return to the levels of pre-Covid, and I can't help but feel for all the lives that were affected by the situation. The debate as to whether all of the Covid actions were necessary, or nothing more than a media & political driven agenda will be waged for years to come. What cannot be debated is that the lives of many good people were forever changed.

Lifelong Friends

In the world of social media, I believe I have somewhere around 400 Facebook connections. Facebook affectionately calls them friends, but are they really friends, or just people you know? Now 400 connections aren't a lot by Social Media standards, where depending on the person, can run up into the thousands, but it seems to be a somewhat fair number of connections. When I look at that number, I often ask myself, how many of those 400 are truly friends? Are they people that I engage with on a regular basis, and genuinely care about what they think, and they in turn offer me the same gifts? If I am truly being honest, that number probably drills down to perhaps 25. So that leaves about 375 people that I am connected with, yet have virtually no connection to. This is not a reflection of any individual who might fall into that category, but rather a recognition that we are close to some people, and not that close to others. It would be simply impossible to have 400 close friends, because at some point, some of those 400 will rise above the others, to become that 25 (your numbers may vary).

So, what happens when the circumstances of 2020 collide with one of those 25? Then you are faced with the very real problem that someone you care for deeply and respect, may be at odds with you and your thoughts and values. The situation is very real, and can happen to anyone as it did me in 2020. Politics, and in this case Covid has no boundaries when it comes to friendships or enemies, it can destroy either if it is allowed to.

My daughter tested positive for Covid-19 in October 2020. Some people when diagnosed as positive choose to run to social media and announce the news. Not really sure why, other than the media had so conditioned people into thinking that it was an instant death sentence, when in fact the science did not support that. My daughter chose to say nothing, a strategy I fully support. Still, no matter how diligent you try to be, somehow things always leak out. She went through her stages and recovered in what seems to be the standard time having tested negative after 12 days. During the last week, I watched the scorn and shunning by people she would consider friends simply because she tested positive, and in some cases had people proceed to tell her how she should be handling it. After 10 days in isolation, she chose to take a walk around our neighborhood block alone, and get some air. Excited that she was feeling better, she shared that event on a Social Media platform, and received several negative feedbacks, by people who have neither experienced it, or have any clue other than media talking points. I'm not really sure if she allowed that experience to sour any of her friendships, or if she just looked at her number, and determined it was not in her 25.

Her experience by extension spilled into my life as well, and had me at a point of considering my options as this did fall within my 25. Earlier in the year, I had started on a walking quest (more on that in the next chapter). This late in the year, and with many people staying home or associating very little with outside family members, I had pretty much relegated myself to walking alone on most of my outings. Gone were the days of me seeing if anyone was interested in an evening walk, and just putting the Air Pods in, and heading out the door. One day towards the end of my daughter's quarantine, she had already been authorized for a return to work, I received a text from a friend asking me if I was going walking. My response was "yes I was planning to go a little later that evening". The response back to me was "I'll meet you at the park". After about a 2-mile walk, the conversation shifted to "what has been going on". Not thinking out of the ordinary, I simply said that my daughter was doing much better now that Covid was gone. That was the point at which this situation went very sideways.

As I mentioned, we did not broadcast her diagnosis as quite frankly, it's no one's business anyway. This included my friend, who upon my disclosure, was not happy that I did not inform him of her condition prior to us going on a walk. Truthfully, since she was past the contagious part, and medically cleared, I never even gave it a thought. This however led to the whole asymptomatic discussion, and a directive that I needed to be tested, because he has a family member that is high risk. To say I was put off by that conversation is an understatement, but what sent me to the point of essentially walking away from this friendship, was an insinuation that I was deliberately negligent in my actions for not disclosing my daughter's condition. There is almost nothing I take more seriously than my loyalty to friends, and there is no way I would ever endanger a person if there was any likely chance that it was a possibility. That is a moral compass that I live by, and now that was being challenged by someone whom I had thought knew me well enough to understand that. As a courtesy to our friendship, I did have a Covid test, and to no surprise the result was negative.

How to move forward after this was the decision I had to make. Each of us has an undetermined threshold that when crossed, we simply refuse to go back and move forward. I knew I was faced with distancing myself from someone who has been a great friend to me, at a time in my life where those are few and far between, or acting as if nothing ever happened. Having some time to think about it did help with some clarity, but I did come to some conclusions. I would let my anger part of the situation go, because I do truly believe that what media and political appointees have been feeding us on a daily basis, is what has everyone in a heightened state, and on edge. But I also determined that I was going to continue to live my life for me, and was not going to start living in fear because it might affect someone else. I take great care in my health, and the necessary precautions I feel are essential for me remaining healthy. There is no doubt this stance will sound selfish to some, and like most everything else in this book, that is their opinion. I am very rarely persuaded by others' opinions, rather choosing to find the facts as they are known in any debate. That is not to say that my mind or ideas can never be changed, but they will not be changed just because someone else says so, especially if they are not part of the 25.

The Covid question certainly took its toll on family, friends and colleagues, and we could be hard pressed to find any silver lining in this situation, but for me, there was a huge silver lining, and a huge life shift for the better. Let's find out just what that was.........

4.

Walking in L.A.
(Nobody walks in L.A.)

There are many things that come to mind when people talk about Southern California. The nice weather, beaches, homelessness, celebrities etc. I didn't say all of the things talked about were nice, because in reality, California has more than its share of negative elements. There is one thing that seems to be universally agreed upon though, and that is Southern California is not considered a place that is ideal for walking. The nature of the landscape, and the never-ending mass of freeways certainly do nothing to dissuade that opinion. So why a chapter devoted solely to walking when I indeed live in Southern California? Well because that dichotomy changed how I live my life, and how I decided to take care of my health, in a way that was a surprise even to me. That last statement may sound a bit melodramatic, but let me tell you how it all got started, and how the success I realized as a result, led me to keep striving for what became a 2-year adventure.

The concept of walking for exercise was not really a new thing that I just happened to discover. There have been several instances over the last couple of years where I would go through periods of walking. Mostly these occurred as I would be planning for an upcoming adventure that would require me to build up my stamina. The first event was a little over 5 years ago when I decided to take a trip to China & Tibet. One of the activities I had planned was a 10 kilometer walk of the Great Wall. This included not just the "restored" section where most tourists go, but a part of the "unrestored" section that very few people go. It was this section that required some uphill hiking and a physical climb of the wall itself. I was also planning a trek to the Base Camp of Mt. Everest in Tibet, that was going to require even more stamina. The trek itself was only about 4 Kilometers, but at an altitude of 17,000 feet, so the oxygen level is about 2/3 of what is normal. In 2019, I traveled to the heart of Russia for a 10-day trip, and while this trip was not as physically challenging, I nonetheless knew that I was going to do a significant amount of walking as a traditional tourist.

My modes operandi for these types of trips would be to start 4 or 5 months in advance and just get used to walking, then after the trip was over, I would stop. I never considered keeping the pace going that I had pre-trip, after I returned. It became just a means to an end, but not something I viewed as a long-term change of lifestyle. For some reason walking is never really viewed as a true form of exercise by most people. Jogging has always held the top spot, or actual weight/cardio training at a gym is what most people see as "true" exercise. In fact, I would guess that if you asked most people, they would probably say walking is boring or is more of an annoyance than something beneficial to physical health. The next time you go to the grocery store, or any store for that matter, watch how many people will sit and wait for a close parking spot to open up, rather than go 10 spaces further, and park right away. OK, I get that sometimes the weather might be bad, and a close space is desirable, but this is Southern California remember, and as Albert Hammond told everyone so eloquently in his 1972 hit song "It Never Rains in Southern California". So, what made walking in 2020 so different for me than in previous years, and how did I totally dispel that myth that nobody walks in L.A.?

The short answer is that there were two elements that changed my focus, and made this my first non-travel adventure of 2020. The first was the Covid-19 pandemic, and the second was the Governor of California. For you see, it was his ridiculous actions in March of 2020 using Covid as his cover to order practically every business closed, and telling everyone that they had to stay home and indoors. I will admit my personality can sometimes have a problem with authority, especially when it is in my opinion excessive. I do have a healthy respect for authority, but as I stated in previous chapters, I felt there was something much more sinister going on with Covid-19, than just a public health concern. I am also an outdoors person, and I knew that there was no way I could remain indoors, and home for an indefinite period of time, based on the word of politicians, and political appointees. Yes, you can close down businesses, but what you can't do is lock me down and prevent me from enjoying the great outdoors. So, I started to walk at one of the local parks as a form of peaceful protest. I have watched on local news for years stories of people demonstrating their Constitutional right to peacefully protest, and now it was my turn!

At first, my protest was pretty basic in that I would go out and walk about 2 miles or so, and call it a night. The mileage itself wasn't really the important part, it was me defying the Governor's wishes, and refusing to stay home that was really driving me. Incidentally, I wasn't the only person engaging in a form of civil disobedience as evidenced by the number of people who were also out walking. With everything essentially shut down, this was all I had as far as entertainment in my life. No, I don't consider sitting home and watching T.V every night as a form of entertainment, and for those who do that's great, but it's not me. So, 5 nights a week for the first two months, I could be found at Santana Park in Corona, (Yeah ironic I know, but that's the name of the city) CA, walking, often on my own.

It's Getting Serious

As March rolled into April, May and now June, for what we were told would be just a 3-week quarantine, I started to wonder just how much walking I had done. So, one evening with more than enough time on my hands, I went back and looked at all the work outs I had done since my start date of March 28th. Not realizing the Walking app I used had a built in calculator for overall work out distances, I manually calculated each work out until I came up with the total. In a little over 2 months, I had walked a total of 119 miles. Not sure why, but seeing that number had me in somewhat of disbelief, as I had not imagined I had walked that much. I knew had a walked a lot, but never really thought it would have reached the century mark. It was that realization, and the fact that lockdowns and closures seemed nowhere near ending anytime soon, that I decided to create some goals around this unexpected new adventure.

I still did not really have a handle on how much walking I was doing, but decided to just establish a goal or a milestone in this case, and see how I would fare. The first goal coincided with my trip to Egypt that was still scheduled to take place in the early part of September 2020. Using my first 2 plus months as the gauge for establishing the next milestone, my target was to reach 250 miles by the time I left for Egypt in September. I felt that was a reasonable goal because I had already proven I could reach that level as long as I stayed committed to the project. What I did not count on was that my commitment turned into almost an obsession to reach this goal. What started out as an average of 2-mile walks, very quickly morphed into anywhere from 3.5 to 5-mile walks, and now as many as 5 or 6 days a week. With this increase in distance and frequency, it became clear to me that I would easily surpass the goal that I had established in June, and indeed by the first 2 weeks in August, I had reached that 250-mile mark, and still had a little more than 2 weeks before I actually left on my trip.

Now that I had reached that milestone, there was no way I was going to just stop until I left for my trip, so I quickly re-calibrated a new goal still keeping the departure date as the timeline. Getting more aggressive, I added a 50-mile rider to the original goal making the new target 300 miles by departure date. This would be a real challenge because I needed to average 25 miles over the next 2 weeks to make it. 2 days before my departure date of September 6th, I crossed the 300-mile threshold with a special guest who joined me on that walk, my daughter Katie.

All of the walking I had done was calculated as dedicated walks, not tracking every step I took throughout the day, like using a pedometer. These were actual exercise walks that I tracked, without any regard to the standard walking I did throughout my day just going through normal routines. With that concept in mind, I never really thought about tracking the walks that I did while I was in Egypt and doing my day long tours that involved significant walking. This included a 14-kilometer hike when I climbed Mt. Sinai for the sunrise view. Also, now that I had reached my journey, in the past the walking would have ended because the goal had been reached, but something was different about this project/adventure, and I never viewed it as something that would end, or at least end right away.

When I returned from Egypt at the end of September, I did not want to lose the momentum that I had gained in the previous 6 months, but felt I needed to establish yet another milestone in order to stay focused and motivated. Based on my current progress, but still wanting to challenge myself with an aggressive goal, a new goal of 500 miles by the end of the year was the new target. I made my goal publicly known through social media as a means of holding myself accountable to make it. If enough people knew about the goal, my fear of not succeeding would be the driving force I needed to ensure my success. It can be very easy to talk yourself out of a goal, when there is no accountability, so I made sure to create that accountability. Once I had the new target in place, and the mechanism to ensure that I stick to the plan, all that was left to do was to actually do the walking.

With my new target in place and well under way, the mental and physical elements I was experiencing were increasing my stamina and desire. 6 months into this project, I had lost over 35 pounds, and at the very start of this next milestone, rocked the scale at 159 pounds. This new-found energy and pride only served to want me to push more, and push I did. I suddenly was averaging over 5 miles each session, and in some cases was pushing 8 or 9 miles. This put me well over 30 and in some cases over 40 miles in one week. I began crushing it, and again knew that I would blow past the 500-mile threshold way before the end of the year. It was right about this time that I had an opportunity to plan a trip to visit Volcan Paricutin in Mexico. This volcano is one of the 7 natural Wonders of the World, and I knew I would get there at some point, but didn't think it would happen so quickly. Thus, the 500-mile milestone was still in play, but I needed to reach that goal before I left for Mexico on November 21st. This would equate to 200 miles in less than 2 months, which was my most ambitious goal to date.

Determined as ever, to make this new adjusted goal, I really pushed the miles, and was easily walking 5 or 6 days each week. Since I knew there was a significant hike that I would be doing in Mexico to reach the volcano, I simulated a hike 2 weeks before departure at the beach, where I did one single walk of 11.5 miles, which was roughly the distance to the volcano and back. Because of that individual hike, and the overall aggressive amounts of walking I was doing, I found myself on the cusp of 500 miles one week before I left for Mexico. In a moment of symbolism, I decided to cross the 500-mile ladder with a short 2 mile walk to the Huntington Beach pier using The Proclaimers song ***"I'm Gonna Be (500 miles)"*** as the theme for the occasion. Just like my other milestones, my oldest daughter Alissa was there to celebrate with me, and to also light our nighttime fire at the beach for smores.

There was still too much time left in the year for this to be the end, right? My thinking exactly, and so the final milestone for the close of what had been a year like no other, was conceived. With 6 weeks left in 2020, I decided to push it to the limit, and finish with a "total miles" walked of 750. This meant I had 6 weeks to walk another 250 miles, by far my most ambitious endeavor, and one that had me questioning my likelihood of success. To make matters even more difficult, I had a surgery on my shoulder to repair some rotator cuff issues, along with the removing of some pieces of clavicle, scheduled for December 17th, and was not sure what type of shape I would be in after that surgery right before the Christmas holiday. I may have bitten off more than I could chew with this last milestone.

Why push this, and not be content with what I had done up to this point? Because for me, the point of the journey is not to arrive, but what you experience along the way. I was going for it, but I also knew I had to get creative in order to make it. My plan was to get 200 miles on the front end of the scheduled surgery, thereby leaving only 50 miles in the final 2 weeks of the year. That meant I needed 200 miles in a little more than 4 weeks, and knew I could not do it simply by allocating exercise time each day. The only way to achieve success was for me to incorporate walking into other aspects of my daily routines. That meant if I needed to pick up a prescription at the pharmacy, I walked to Rite Aid to pick it up, which allowed me to add 3 miles into the mix. I started walking during my lunch time, and in some cases walking to pick up lunch. If I could afford the time, I was walking to address any errands I needed to complete.

I engaged myself in a project to scour the local neighborhoods in search of unique Christmas displays which took me out of my normal walking paths, and into other areas that actually increased my walking distances. Talking with total strangers in these new neighborhoods, I found myself racking up the miles, and embracing that ever elusive "Christmas Spirit" along the way. December 16th was a pivotal night since it was the night before my surgery, but also the night of a 4.6 mile walk that pushed me within 50 miles of the magical 750-mile mark. I was on target, and where I wanted to be, but still facing a surgery, and an unknown physical fitness to complete this 9-month adventure.

The surgery went well on December 17th, and my goal of taking a short walk on the 18th was realized, although I clearly had a lack of energy. I knew that I would not be able to do the long walks, and had to shift my strategy to 2 shorter walks per day. There I was that first week of surgery walking to Dunkin Donuts with coffee in one arm, and a sling on the other arm. It didn't matter when it was, if I could fit a walk in, I was going to. That included a late afternoon Christmas Eve walk to Rite Aid for a refill on pain medication. I was too close to the goal not to make it a reality, and that first week after surgery, I was not in top form, but kept going. Once the doctor took out the stitches, and told me to lose the sling, I had a bit more mobility, but was still struggling with stamina. Finally, on the afternoon of December 30th, I finished the project in fitting style with 5.2 mile walk to close out 2020 with a total of 752 miles walked, and a new pair of shoes. What started out 9 months earlier as my own personal protest, ended with a test of my will, commitment, and a renewed sense of focus on maintaining better health. As the pandemic nonsense continued throughout 2021, periods of opening up and closing down ensued as did my walking. The year 2021 saw me walk an additional 1175 miles, which was 25 miles short of my January 1st goal.

What I Learned

Probably the most asked question I had along the way was how did I stay focused and what kept me from getting bored with just walking. There is no doubt that the standard practice of walking doesn't seem very exciting, but each of us has our own way of finding that interest. For me, walking became very therapeutic, and a chance for me to quietly unwind. My personality requires that I need to have quiet time, which allows me to be more creative. Much of what you will read in this book was conceived while I was doing many of these walks. Ideas would pop into my head, and I would expand on those ideas while adding to the overall miles. Walking through several parks and having a chance to view youth sports activities (when they were allowed) gave me hope that things would return to a somewhat normal state, although I really didn't know when. Also, the loss of weight, and the overall effect on how I felt physically, and mentally was a huge key in the effort to stay focused. There were countless days when I just wasn't motivated to walk, but forced myself out there, and was glad I did later on.

I think the number one aid people often use for exercise motivation is music, and I am as guilty of that as anyone. Music is as much engrained in my life as anything else I can think of. So, when I am walking solo, which is most of the time, it is my constant companion. It was not uncommon for me to put in the Air Pods or Beats, and simply slip into my own world of "Rock Star", without any awareness of my true environment. This has been on display many times, and I can say with the utmost confidence that more than one eyebrow has been raised when I would forget where I was on a Sunday morning, and let out the high notes of the last chorus of Bon Jovi's "Runaway". I can only imagine what other park goers are wondering when the likes of me walks past belting out AC/DC with my air guitar, or a Neil Peart drum solo matching him note for note on my air drums (see chapter 1). Humans are very quick to judge, especially when you are not conforming to what they think you should, and that can be daunting at times. But what I really learned through all of this is that I can establish my own goals, stay committed to them, appreciate the benefits of that commitment, and stay true to who I am. I also learned that somebody walks in L.A.

One of my many evening walks
(Santana Park, Corona, CA

5.

Cruel Summer

Things had started to get very serious as this pandemic thing rolled into June of 2020, and now some of my adventure goals became disrupted. Up to this point, the pandemic was mostly a mild inconvenience to me, while others were still paralyzed by fear. I discovered a new passion for walking and exercise, so that was all good, and my overall travel plans were still intact, but things were getting a bit dicey. A couple of work-related trips that I was going to attach some fun to, had been canceled, and while I was disappointed, my main adventure still slated a few months away could not possibly be canceled, or could it. The opportunity to visit Yellowstone National Park in the Spring went South, and I had just learned that a Conference in Denver for July had the plug pulled on it, so that ruined what would have been my 1st visit to Mount Rushmore in South Dakota. Yes, what was starting to be a cruel summer was only just beginning.

Covid Hits Home

The constant barrage of media and their death counts on a daily basis became almost mind numbing, and if ever I started to feel desensitized, it was now during the summer time. While I had heard of some acquaintances who has experienced death within their family that was Covid related, I personally did not know anyone directly connected to me. That is until my Mother-in-Law Eileen passed away at the end of June 2020. Eileen was a wonderful person in my life, and even though my life had traveled down a path that ended in divorce, she continued to treat me as her Son-in-Law. Eileen did not pass away from the Covid-19 virus, but the devasting lockdowns and government overreach took their toll on her quality of life. Unable to see her family and spend time with her grandchildren proved to be too much for her. With no real end to the nonsense being sanctioned as government mandates, her desire to continue living life on someone else's terms waned, and she appeared to give up. Her loss was particularly difficult for me as she was very much a mother to me, especially after my mother passed away 5 years earlier. Eileen left behind a legacy of kindness and faith that the Pope himself would have a hard time duplicating, and she is missed by all who knew her.

Walking on Air

Determined to not let these latest events spoil my adventure plans, I had to pivot in some way to salvage what was quickly becoming a very depressing start to the summer season. With Mount Rushmore now gone, and my mood feeling a bit defeated, I wanted to do something to prove that this pandemic would not stop me from enjoying this year. Air travel was tenuous at best, and many places still remained closed, so I had no idea what I could do, and still not compromise my standards of having fun. Whatever I was going to do, it had to fall in the category of something more local, than extreme. But what if I could find something to do that was maybe a little of both. A quick look through my last book under the chapter of North America in the "What's Left" section gave me my answer.

For quite some time I had always wanted to see the Sky Walk at the Grand Canyon West Rim, but just never found myself heading in that direction. I had been to the South Rim of the Canyon a couple of times, but I was really intrigued by the Sky Walk, that was built out over the Canyon, and knew this was the time to give it try. Logistics worked out as it is only about a 6-hour drive to Kingman Arizona, and the 4th of July long week end was coming up, so the opportunity was presented before me, and I took it. Because Covid killed the tourism industry, entrance fees and sightseeing tours were at an all-time low. While many people were moaning on social media that they had to cancel vacations, I was determined to take an unexpected mini vacation, and take it, I did.

A hot summer drive through the desert was a serene feeling as it was just me, my semi new car, and rock n roll to sing my way to Arizona. Traveling parts of the journey along the famous Route 66 added a bit of the nostalgia for what would be my first travel adventure of 2020. I made it to Kingman for the night, and managed to secure a decent rate at a Comfort Inn that I would call home for 2 nights, then made my way into the Downtown area for some dinner. I knew it wouldn't be a late night, as I had an early start planned for the Sky Walk, and an added surprise that I decided to make happen at the last minute.

The sky walk itself was a bit anticlimactic but still an architectural marvel when you think about it. Just one more opportunity for me to challenge that nasty fear of heights I have, and to experience something new. Like most things though, there always seems to be a catch in the enjoyment, and the Sky Walk was no different. This was actually my first trip where I had a chance to break out my new high end digital camera. With my colossal failure of photographing the Aurora Borealis with a basic iPhone a few months earlier, I made a commitment to improving my photography skills, and upgrading my equipment was the start of that. Armed with my new camera, and the Go Pro, I soon found out that personal photography equipment was not allowed out on the bridge. So that meant no pictures of the canyon from 100 or so feet out into the wide open, would come from me. However, if I wanted to pay, their photographer would be happy to take a variety of poses and views, which would be on sale in the gift shop upon my departure. In the end, I did purchase a small package, and made the most of the views I was able to capture with my own equipment. After numerous hiking trails and rock climbs to get some amazing footage of both still shots and video for my YouTube channel, and feeling the effects of the now 100+ degree day, it was time for a break, and to get ready for another first in the afternoon

My motto has always been to "go big or go home" and this adventure was no different. That meant that just visiting the Sky Walk wasn't going to be enough. Of the many height challenges I have put myself through, one that has alluded me has been a helicopter ride. That was going to change, when at the last minute, I decided to look into a helicopter ride over the Canyon. This is a very popular tourist event, and one of the more expensive tours you can take in this area. But like so many other sightseeing adventures that were struggling because of Covid, the prices were greatly reduced, so I made sure to strike while the iron, or in this case, the sun was hot! So off I went with a group of about 4 other people flying in a helicopter over the canyon, and actually landing down inside right along the Colorado river. This allowed me to have a crash course in temperature change as the top of the Canyon was a balmy 100 degrees, but down inside at the river basin, it was an unbearable 120 degrees, but hey, it's a dry heat. Flying back out of the Canyon and an additional 15-minute flight was the end to an incredible day of nature made phenomena, and a chance to head back to the hotel for some much-needed air conditioning, for the next day was a return home to California.

The "A" Lister

The long holiday week end at the Grand Canyon was somewhat of a reprieve from the cruel Summer as I got to at least do a small adventure, and the big adventure for September was still on the books, although starting to feel a bit tenuous. But as life often provides balance, for every good thing, there often seems to be something that is not so good. If my travel life was severely impacted because of lockdowns, one can only imagine the toll a personal life can take. At first, all this family togetherness, and time to reflect on family time, and dinners together made for great theater, played out on the nightly news. But little thought is often given to the single person, who perhaps has grown children off on their own adventures, and no significant other to speak of. As a single man, the dating world is often hard enough under the best of circumstances, but shut down any form of social interaction outside of the home, and you have the makings of a very difficult and yes often lonely existence.

During this time, social media use increased exponentially, much to the delight of many of the most socially awkward individuals who created it. It's no secret of my disdain for the whole social media concept, however, I will concede that part of social media has played a very important role in my life, in that it allowed me to re-connect with many people whom I grew up with. Like anything else in the world, the good qualities of social media can often mutate into less desirable elements, and that's where I tend to get off the train. It was in that context that I found myself chatting with a longtime friend from my neighborhood. During the course of the conversation, I mentioned how difficult being single was and that next "love" seemed to be very illusive. She mentioned to me that a friend of hers had been experiencing similar situations. She asked me if I remembered this person, and I was shocked to find that the person she was referring to was in fact single and struggling as well. This was not someone I would have imagined having any issues in the relationship/marriage department. A broken or failed marriage can happen to anyone, but it is assumed most people are able to start over again at some level.

This particular person was someone whom I would refer to as an "A" lister. I knew her in high school, but did not really know her. She was not someone I would have considered even approaching back in the day, simply because we did not play in the same sand box. I have written in past books about my awkward high school years, and the lack of self-confidence that dogged me all those years ago, and perhaps to this day still does. At the suggestion of my friend, I decide to reach out in a very informal way. A friend request, became an accept, became some private messages back and forth, and a sharing of history since the early 1980's. As I heard her story, I could not help but see the similarities of circumstances, and thus began to feel empathy and understanding.

The thought of "did I really want to go down this long-distance road" thing again crossed my mind, but I'll admit I was consumed by my flashback, that one the prettiest, and most popular girls in high school, actually showed an adult interest in me. The conversations continued, and many were about the logistics, how would things work, and some even a bit more risqué. But even more glaring were the conversations that went from one end of the spectrum to the other. Where a conversation on a Monday ended with "this can never work, we should not continue to try" to the next day asking why she hadn't heard from me. It became clearer with each passing day, that this was not the right fit, and yet after each apology message, I found myself extending the benefit of the doubt. The communication in one form or another continued for about 2 months, until things bordered on the bizarre, and I finally stated that I no longer wished to communicate in any form, and to no longer contact me. I know that my line in the sand was the right decision to make, but in the end, it didn't make me feel any better, or change the overall situation of my personal life. Rather, it was just another blow to the male ego. Surely this was the low point of the cruel Summer, or was it?

Grand Canyon Skywalk
July, 2020

Grand Canyon Helicopter Ride
July, 2020

6.

Walk Like an Egyptian

All of the impediments to life through the first 7 months of 2020 amounted to little more than annoyances, but things were now starting to get really scary. For you see, my main adventure of 2020 had seriously become in jeopardy. A trip that I had mapped out with complete intricacy, was on the very cusp of canceling within 30 days of my departure, and for a brief time, did in fact cancel. If this turn of events played out, I was going to be devasted. Now that might sound a bit melodramatic, but you have to remember, traveling is a huge part of my life under normal circumstances. Take away most of the standard functions of life by closing public venues, wearing ridiculous masks when you leave your home, and being pretty much reduced to take out fast food, and there isn't a whole lot left for a single person. During this whole event, my single focus had been about this next adventure I was going to take. A chance to touch my 6th continent as well as the realization of seeing places that I learned so much about as a child in Sunday school.

Before I go into the problem, I should probably provide some context to the actual buildup of what would become known as *"The Egyptian Adventure"*. In January of 2020, after I returned from the Arctic Circle of Alaska, I started planning what my 2020 true adventure would be. For some time, I had on my radar a trip to the Middle East, mostly what is often called or referred to as "The Holy Land". Through a variety of political and military turmoil's that has encompassed this area since long before I was born, I tried to make a trip to Egypt & Israel happen on several occasions, but things just never fell into place. I came across an incredible airfare in and out of Cairo from Los Angeles, and thought this is my moment. As happens in so many instances, when I find a good travel deal, I will often pull the trigger, and not have all the elements thought through. In the airfare game, if you don't strike right away, the deal could be gone, and I did not want to miss out on this. So, I purchased tickets to Cairo Egypt, and now all I had to do was figure out what I was going to do.

The more research I did, the more I wanted to add into this upcoming adventure. This is not uncommon for me, and in fact, most trips I plan, always end up adding extra things or places beyond what was the original scope. As I started to do my research for Egypt, I had several key points I had to touch. Then realizing just how close I was to the country of Jordan, I just had to figure out a way to see the lost city of Petra. Hell, now that I was going to be so close to Israel, let's make a few extra days in Jerusalem happen, and a chance to experience all of the stories or the Old & New Testament of the Bible. The more research I did, the more I wanted to see & do. About a month after I bought my ticket, I was able to contact a business contact at Delta Airlines, who was able to help me change my flights, which would now allow me to fly to Cairo, but home from Tel Aviv Israel. This would save me a full day's travel back to Egypt, along with the hassles of transiting 3 countries to get back to Cairo airport.

Open the Borders

The logistics of the trip were confirmed when the first wave of Covid hit in March of 2020. As has been mentioned in earlier chapters, I was always skeptical of the gloom & doom scenario that the media and government were peddling to a worldwide audience. I felt surely this would blow over in a couple of weeks, because remember, we just needed to "flatten the curve". Remember when that was the goal, and we would solve the problem? As the months piled up, I soon found myself in July, and while Egypt had continued to go about its business, Israel & Jordan were locked up tighter than a drum. I kept checking with tour operators that I had bookings with, and each time, they kept saying, "things were ready to open up". Well, they didn't, and I was on the precipice of having my one big adventure for the year cancel on me, and I was not happy.

The floor pretty much fell out from under me at about 30 days before I was scheduled to leave. At this point, I gave up on the Israel Jordan portion of the trip, and had to focus my energies on just staying within Egypt. I decided since I basically had 5 extra days to now account for, I would turn my attention to Southern Egypt. So, I rerouted the trip to include stops in Aswan & Luxor Egypt. I was able to confirm some tours, booked the air flights, and found a couple of great hotels at rock bottom prices. Right at the moment the new trip was all confirmed, the final nail seemed to be ready for my Egyptian coffin. I had already had a couple of my international flights change on me, but 30 days before I was scheduled to leave, Air France decided to cancel their service into Cairo. So, both KLM and Air France had canceled their service and I was left with no way to get to Egypt. At this point I was pretty much burned out on the whole process. Every obstacle that you could imagine had been thrown into my path, and I had given up almost all hope of this trip happening. My nature has always been if I want something bad enough, I will not give up, and continue to work for it. There were two things that were really driving my tenacity. The 1st was that I really wanted to take the trip, and the 2nd was a few naysayers out there did not believe I was going to be able to go. I was not going to be driven by Covid hysteria, and would do all possible to fight against the odds and travel internationally during what was known as a pandemic. My only challenge, I still had no way to actually get to Egypt.

Rule 240

Somewhat resigned to thinking my trip was canceled left me deflated, and in fact I remember thinking what other alternative trips could I take to fill this vacation time slot. It was right at this time that I decided I was due to write another book about this whole silly pandemic nightmare, and what the effects were to someone who travels for a career and pleasure. I recall heading to the beach to make a video announcing this new book project, and in the video, I included a clip about my canceled trip to Egypt. It was not long after that, when my career in the travel industry allowed me to recall a tiny piece of legislation that would save my trip. Enter the little-known rule 240. This is a piece of airline regulation that essentially states, if the airline has a significant delay, or cancelation, they are required by law to make some element of compensation to the passenger. This can be in the form of another flight on the same or different carrier, or provide the passenger a refund. Air France canceling the flight, fell into that category. So, I called Delta Airlines, which is who I booked my ticket through a joint venture agreement they have with Air France, and I told them I wanted to cancel the flight. They immediately went into their, your $700.00 will be on credit for a future flight, when I advised them that Air France canceled the flight, and I was entitled to a full refund of the ticket, and that is what I wanted. Before I called, I had already done my homework and found a Lufthansa flight that was able to get me in and out of Cairo. So, I took my Delta refund, and purchased a brand-new ticket on Lufthansa. In the end, the new ticket cost me about $50.00 more, but the trip was back on! The average person is generally not aware of their rights when it comes to matters of interrupted travel. The airline will not openly tell you, because they do not want you to do what I did. They want you to continue to fly with them, and not take your money to another airline. Having that industry knowledge was certainly a benefit to me in this circumstance, and was the loop hole I needed to do the "Egyptian Adventure".

Departure day arrived, and against all the odds and the naysayers, I was on my way to the airport. But the departure day wasn't without its last-minute drama. The day before I was set to leave, I had to take a Covid test, and 1 hour before my appointment, the facility called me and told me the machine was broken, and they had to cancel my appointment, or book me to another facility. Fortunately, I was able to find another location about 40 miles away, took the test, and got the results in 30 minutes. Testing services for travel at this time were still relatively new, so there were not a lot of options, so this was just one more hurdle to overcome. Arriving at the international terminal at LAX was surreal, as it was basically a ghost town. Almost every store was closed, and there could not have been more than 100 people in the whole building. As crazy as it had all been, I was soon on my way to Frankfurt Germany where I would connect to a flight that would take me on to Egypt.

My layover in Frankfurt was about 11 hours, so as I always do whenever possible, I decided to take a trip into the city. I love that almost all European airports have a train service that takes you into the heart of the city, and Frankfurt was no different. Walking around the city on a beautiful September day was the perfect time kill, along with a few pints, and giant soft pretzels with mustard. Arriving back at the airport, I arrived at the Cairo gate, and witnessed every sob story possible by passengers, who did not have the proper test results to enter Egypt. Travel had certainly changed, for there was a new sheriff in town, and his name was Covid. A late-night arrival in Cairo went very smooth, and soon I found myself in a hotel room overlooking the Great Pyramids of Giza. I was about to partake on a history lesson, that no professor or high school teacher could have equaled.

Cairo

Having planned this trip for about 9 months, I had done a tremendous amount of research on the things I wanted to do, and watched a lot of YouTube videos of other people's travel to Egypt. Based on many recommendations, I decided to hire a local guide whom I learned about through a service called Guru Walks. This is a tip-based service of local guides offering tours within major cities. I often like to do a combination of actual guided tours, and independent small group tours, where I have more flexibility to explore on my own. Each circumstance is unique, but for this trip, I felt it best to have a bit more structure. The guide of the tour I had signed up for sent me a direct message, introduced himself, and provided me with additional information that without a doubt, made my trip more memorable. Because tourism was almost completely dead from Covid, I was the only person he had scheduled for his tours. His name was Sherif Abdelhameed, and I ended up hiring him as my private guide for my 3 full days in Cairo.

Day 1 had me at the Giza Pyramids, and the history lesson was on. Sherif explained the history, and the religious implications of ancient Egypt. We visited the 3 main pyramids of the complex, saw the sphinx, and he even arranged a camel ride for me. It was during this time I realized the value of having a local guide with me, as he properly negotiated, and shielded me from the vendors. Egyptian vendors, especially at tourist sights, are notorious for being very aggressive, sometimes to the point of downright annoying. Because of his presence, I felt much less intruded on as I viewed structures that were built 3500 years ago. In addition to his wealth of knowledge, he was also an amazing photographer. Because I often travel solo, I find a lot of times if I want a picture with some famous landmark, I usually have to ask a complete stranger, or by pass the photo altogether. The hot sun, and the jet lag had kicked in from my 1st day, so it was a short walk back to my hotel, and plenty of time to rest for the amazing pyramid light show which I watched from my balcony, to cap off an amazing day.
The 2nd day had Sherif taking me to the Mediterranean coastal city of

Alexandria. A lot of people opt to by-pass this city, but I wanted to see it because of its rich Roman history as the city was named after Alexander the Great. True to form, the architecture of this city was very much Roman, and it boasts one of the worlds 1st known libraries. The Library of Alexandria was well known for housing some of the 1st scholarly work of the world's greatest thinkers. Touring the catacombs, the Roman amphitheater, and the Citadel, which used to be the ancient lighthouse made for a full day. Having absorbed so much history, and amazing architecture over the first 2 days, a case could be made for a little break. There was no time however, as I only had 1 additional day in Cairo, and that was allocated for some culture and shopping.

 I have had an opportunity in my lifetime to visit many of the world's greatest museums, such as the Louvre in Paris, The Smithsonian in Washington DC, and the Hermitage in St. Petersburg Russia. So, a chance to add the Egyptian Museum in Cairo would not be squandered. Sherif had me ready to go bright and early, as it's always better to beat the crowds, and the museum was not air conditioned, and temperatures would be well over 100 degrees today. Several hours seeing the exhibits of ancient Egyptian, the process of mummification, and the King Tut exhibit were mind blowing. I only hope I can return to see the new Grand Egyptian Museum which has now opened in the Giza Plateau, replacing the original museum. We still had some shopping to do, so off we went to the Khan el Khalili Bizarre. This is a famous market for tourists to buy souvenirs and many other items, along with some great street food. Sherif's negotiation skills were put to the test again as I had a list of people that I needed to get some trinkets for. Shopping, lunch, and an afternoon coffee rounded out the day, as it was time to prepare for my departure to the next part of Egypt. Having Sherif as my personal guide made my trip complete, and the only way I could think of to properly thank him, was to refer his services onward. In 2021, some friends that I had met in China, wanted to go to Egypt, largely based on the videos from my trip, and they hired Sherif as their guide. I continue to have him produce videos for me for my YouTube channel, and am proud to call him my friend.

Crossing the Red Sea

If you asked the average traveler where some of the best beaches or scuba diving can be found, I doubt many would respond with the Red Sea. Strange as it may sound, that is exactly what I would discover, as phase

2 of the Egyptian Adventure would take me to the Sinai Peninsula, and the resort city of Sharm el Sheikh. People from the West are not all that familiar with this area, and unfortunately, because of where it is located, many people avoid this area. The Sinai Peninsula conjures up many images, mostly negative from main stream media, of political instability, and Middle East wars of the past. This area is not unlike other places where there are dangerous areas, and perfectly safe areas. Now I could have chosen a lot of places to go if my goal was water & beaches, but Sharm el Sheikh had one other element that was high on my list.

Ever since my trip to Mt. Everest in 2017, I have become fixated with mountains and adventure climbing. So, when I learned that "Sharm" was a gateway to being able to climb Mt. Sinai, that became a must do. When I first arrived, I wanted to take things a bit easy, so I decided to book a couple of water activities. People will often ask me, "do I ever do anything fun on these adventures" immediately equating water, sun and sand as the equivalent to fun. For me, all adventure is fun, whether climbing, walking through history, and yes, a great day in the water. Since I was on the Red Sea, I decided to book some water fun, that included parasailing, a tube ride, and something called a banana boat ride. Parasailing was the big attraction, although I had done this before in the Caribbean, it had been 30 years, so a refresher was in order. Add to that, my GoPro camera was going to allow me to film from a much different perspective. I spent 3 hours enjoying the Red Sea, meeting some very nice people, and filming my parasailing experience. Some rest was needed, because what I had planned later was going to require a lot of stamina on my part.

Up till now, my Egyptian Adventure consisted mostly of traditional tourist related activities, but that was going to change. Because now, I was going to hike to the top of Mt. Sinai to watch the sunrise. For those who may not be familiar with the biblical lore, Mt. Sinai is believed to be the location where Moses received the 10 commandments from God. To be fair, there is a debate whether this is the real location or another location in Saudi Arabia. I'm not going to discuss that here, as this location has claimed to be the site for a long period time, and that's good enough for me. Mt. Sinai aka Mt. Horeb is located near the town of St. Catherine's. This is located about 3 hours ride from Sharm el Sheikh by bus. The schedule was to leave around 9:30pm, start the hike up the mountain around 1:00a, and arrive at the top in time for sunrise. Climbing a mountain in the dead of night might not be everyone's cup of tea, but for a Mid Life Adventurer, this was a perfect fit.

The bus ride into the Sinai desert did take about 3 hours, but soon we arrived at the Monastery of St. Catherine's. We received some instruction about the hike, and met our official Bedouin guide who would walk the trail in the dark with the group. There were many different tour groups that converged on the mountain for this hike, but there were about 8 people that were actually in my group. The base was very well lit with flood lights to ensure everyone got off on the right path, but soon we were walking the trail, and as we ascended, things started to get much darker. Even with my hiking headlamp, the pitch dark brought on a sense of foreboding as we continued to climb. Well out of any ambient light, the night sky lit up like a Christmas tree with all of the stars now fully overhead.

After about 45 minutes of pretty traditional hiking paths, with very little grade to them, the terrain significantly changed. For you see, the rest of the hike would consist of over 700 stone steps. Not the traditional steps of a stair case, but a path that contained steps every 3 or 4 feet. Probably around half way to the top, we came across a rest place complete with sodas, candy & chips, and surprisingly even beer. Even in the remotest places, one can still find good ole fashioned capitalism. I remember thinking that I now realized why it took Moses over 40 days to climb the mountain, because he apparently stopped for a Coke & Kit Kats. At around 4:30am, we arrived at the last rest stop at the base of the summit. There was only a 100-step stair case, and we would be at the top of Mt. Sinai to witness the sunrise, that was due in about 55 minutes. Since the temperature had dropped considerably, I took the opportunity to change my sweaty shirt, into a nice dry & warm hoodie.

I arrived at the summit with about 15 minutes before the sun would start to rise. For this moment I decided to use a new zoom lens I got for my camera, to give me a variety of focal ranges. It became light before the actual sunrise, and it gave me the opportunity to see for the first time, the surrounding mountain ranges, and just how far we had climbed through the night. The 360-degree view was incredible, and a sense of achievement befell me, as this was another of these unique summits that I have been able to witness. Soon the sun peaked over the horizon, and the sound of camera shutters going off became unmistakable. This was a moment that had been long planned, and highly anticipated by me, and yet, it almost didn't happen.

After about 30 minutes at the top, the major event was technically over, but we now had the inevitable descent. Climbing back down in the day light was considerably easier, and a lot quicker, but this was still the desert, and in no time the temperature would hit 90 degrees by 6:30am. Walking back down the mountain, I picked up the pace, and ventured ahead of the rest of the group. It took me about 90 minutes to descend back down to the monastery, where shade and water were plentiful. This truly was a mid-life adventure for me, and one that I am glad I took the time to experience. Having been awake for over a 24-hour period, and still staring a 3-hour bus ride back to Sharm el Sheikh, I knew that a well-deserved sleep was in order.

Ancient Egypt

After what became a 15-hour nap, it was time to start traveling again and depart the Red Sea resort city. It was at this point of the trip where I had to change itineraries because of Covid. My original plan at inception would have been to leave the Red Sea and travel to the country of Jordan, and on to Israel, however, since those countries did not open the borders, I made other arrangements to head to Upper Egypt. This meant I was flying to the city of Aswan, and would continue to what was in reality the capital of Ancient Egypt, the city of Luxor. It was also the first time I would experience a disruption in my altered plans, again thanks to Covid.
All of my previous adventures have had very little issues or changes to the itinerary, because I spend a huge amount of time mapping out the strategy, and making sure everything was confirmed, and setup. However, Egypt Air decided to be the first, of what I would soon discover to be a variety of changes, cancelations, and flat out denied entry in my future travels.

Egypt Air delayed my flight from Sharm el Sheikh just enough that I misconnected in Cairo with my flight to Aswan. Since there was only 1 flight a day to Aswan, I could not get there until the next day. I only had 1 day in Aswan, so I decided to spend the night in Cairo, and fly to Luxor the next day. This meant I was going to miss my tour to the Temples of Abu Simbel, and a chance to see the High Dam, along with some Nile crocodiles. Since I was spending 3 nights in Luxor, it just made sense to skip that part of the trip, and resume as scheduled the next day. A few phone calls to the hotel and tour operator, and everything was adjusted, and I was very grateful that both hotel and tour operator were understanding and completely refunded my money.

I arrived in Luxor midafternoon, and proceeded to the Hilton hotel sitting right on the Nile River. This was the nicest, most Western style hotel in the city, and the price was a whopping $48.00 per night. The next 2 days would be jammed pack, so any rest I had planned would be on day 1, so I put the time to good use, and enjoyed the massive swimming pool, and pool bar service. Dinner at the outdoor hotel restaurant with my table literally 10 feet away from the river, was an incredible experience, and gave me just a piece of the Western lifestyle that had been missing for the first 8 days of the trip. It wouldn't be long before the history lessons would start again.

The city of Luxor is defined by the East bank and the West Bank of the Nile River. The East represents life, and the West represents death (afterlife). The temples that are built there reflect that philosophy, but on this day, we would experience it all. First stop on the tour was the Karnak Temple, and then on to the Luxor Temple. Both of these temples are dedicated to the life of the Pharaohs, and were used as places of worship. Karnak had an amazing number of columns and obelisks, all containing the hieroglyphics on each one. I remember being so blown away by the restoration work that had been done to preserve these writings. Some of these dating as far back as 4000 years, sitting right in the middle of a major city. Luxor Temple was filled with the stone statues of Pharaohs, and other Gods. The most impressive thing was the sheer size and the carvings within the stone.
A quick lunch, and it was on to the West bank of the city to Queen Hatshepsut's Temple. I always have to pronounce that name slowly to say it right. This was a Temple that was cut out of a mountain into an impressive structure. It was here that I would meet an amazing young

man named Akram. He is from the Luxor area, and was visiting the temple with some friends. He heard me speaking to my guide, and walked up to me while I was filming, and asked if he could take a picture with me. I wasn't sure what he wanted at first, but then realized he wanted to be in a picture with me. My guide snapped a couple of photos, and he gave me his "WhatsApp" information and asked if I could send him the pictures. This young man is a dedicated college student, and I am proud to say, we still talk via social media. He is another example of someone that I have met during my international travels that I call a friend. I would very soon find this to be a trend with Egyptian people.

The final stop for the day would be the Valley of the Kings. This is the place where the tombs of many of the Pharaohs were buried, including the famous King Tut. Only some of the tombs are open for viewing, but the paintings and writings inside of these tombs was spectacular. The thriving societies that existed thousands of years ago was beyond what my imagination could fathom. Sadly, the elements of modern society have seeped into this site, as care takers inside the tombs will literally shake you down looking for tips, to a level of almost forcing. They want to take pictures, and want tipped for every picture they take. It was a very stressful scene, and as a result, I limited the number of tombs I would actually visit. This would not take away from a very full, incredible, and an exceptionally hot day in Luxor.

The Journey Home

The journey home from Egypt would be a long one that started with a 10-hour train ride from Luxor back to Cairo. As I rode along the Nile Valley, I had a chance to see the challenging part of Egypt. This is a country of 100 million people, and there are many who do not have what we in the West consider "the basics". Over the course of 10 days, I had seen so many wonderful sites, eaten some amazing local food, and met some of the kindest people you could ever meet. Yet, there is this part that we don't want to think about, the "have's" and the "have nots". Every stereo type I had built into my psyche, every bullshit story seen on CNN or other media outlets that tell us Muslim countries hate Americans, and all the other misnomers, were staring me in the face on that long train ride back to Cairo. The question "can one man make a difference" is often asked.

Whether the answer is yes or no depends on your perspective I guess, but what isn't in doubt is that "one can sure try".

On my way home, I started communicating with a young man named Ahmed Soliman, He is from the Sohag region, which is just a little North of Luxor. Ahmed is like many of the young men I met there, college students wanting to make their country a better place. They are very excited to meet and talk with Americans, because they don't have the opportunity to do so very often. When I returned home, I tried to think of ways I could help him with his goal of coming to college in America. I started helping him with advice on applying to schools, and wrote a recommendation letter for him to support his college application. We talk on a regular basis, and he always checks in to see how I am doing. He has had a difficult life for a young man of 24 years, and yet he has the best and most positive attitude I have seen in any young person. My sister had often wanted me to become involved in the "Big Brothers" program, because she felt I was good with kids. Well, it took a me a little longer than I thought, but I believe I joined the "International Big Brothers" program, and it has made me a better person.

Pyramids & Sphinx of Giza
Giza, EG. September, 2020

Sunset on the Nile River
Luxor, EG. September, 2020

The light show at the Great Pyramids
Giza, EG. September, 2020

The Citadel of Alexandria
Alexandria, EG. September, 2020

Standing atop Mt. Sinai
Saint Catherine, EG. September, 2020

Inside a Pharaoh's tomb, Valley of the Kings
Luxor EG. September, 2020

7.

Everyday I Write the Book

With this being my 4th book, writing was not a new endeavor for me, but one that has opened up a new means of communicating. Writing became another avenue that allowed me to share my thoughts with a larger audience, or essentially anyone who was willing to listen. For a very long time, I had a goal or dream if you will, that I wanted to write a book. I believe that everyone has a story in them, but most people don't believe they have the means to tell that story. With the advent of self-publishing, it made writing & publishing a book, that much more attainable for the average person. I include myself in that large category of self-published authors.

I never viewed my writing and publishing a book as a career pivot, or as a means of making significant income that would allow me to alter my life course, but rather a personal achievement goal. That is not to say that if I had written a book that became a "best seller", I would be upset with myself, but my main motivation was always personal achievement. If people managed to find my words interesting or even better, helpful in some way, that would be more than enough satisfaction to consider what I had done to be a success. But something happened along the way between my last book, and the formulation of this book, that would make my writing far more worthwhile, than any amount of money could bring me.

I can't think of anything more satisfying to me than to be able to inspire others. For many years now, I have been regularly telling people to live life now, go on an adventure, do the things you want to do now, and most importantly, to stop waiting to do them. I have communicated this consistent message through various social media outlets including a Facebook Author page, my personal Facebook page, and my YouTube channel, Mid Life Adventures. All in an attempt to inspire others to seek their dreams. But it was my writing that would afford me the opportunity to inspire others more than those other mediums combined, and I was about to find out how.

Right before I left for Egypt in early September of 2020, I received a private message on my Facebook Author Page, and it was probably one of the greatest messages I have ever received. I opened the message and literally could not believe what I had read. To wit:

Hi

<u>This fall</u> I have the pleasure of teaching Tourism (remotely) at MassBay Community College in Wellesley, MA. In place of a textbook (which many students opt out of reading), I am having the students read your book –On Top of the World and Cassie De Pecol's book – Expedition 196. Hopefully, your words will inspire the students to dream and discover a world of education outside of the classroom.

I love to invite guest speakers into the classroom. <u>This fall</u> I am doing this remotely through a pre-recorded Zoom conversation. I send questions to the speakers ahead of time. I would love to have the students "meet you". I am hoping you have a little time to talk with me about your philosophy of travel and your career in the travel industry. I look forward to hearing from you.

After reading the message a few times, I felt a little strange, and while I was flattered, I was more skeptical. It's not uncommon to receive solicitations from a variety of different people wanting to *"boost my followers"* or *"increase my search optimization"* all for a fee of course. At that moment I really wasn't sure what to think. I quickly reached out to my friend Matt Hausmann, whose career has been spent in the education technology space. I shared the message with him and point blank asked him "do you think this is legit". Shame on me for not having enough faith in my own work, that I would immediately discount the voracity of this message, but I have had too many wealthy lost cousins from Nigeria, to take just any unsolicited message on faith.

Within a few minutes Matt confirmed that the message was indeed legitimate as the sender, Roberta Allison is an instructor at Mass Bay Community College in the Boston area. Could this really be true? Was my book going to be required reading in a college course dealing with subject matter that I have acquired over 35 years of experience in? A topic that I have been so adamant about, and encouraging my personal inner circle of connections to seek? A chance to reach an entire new generation of youth, and inspire them to live the experiences that I have lived? The answer to all these questions was yes, and I was going to have a chance to present my case, in my words.

The Zoom Reality

As Roberta explained in her initial message to me, the process was normally to have guest speakers come into the classroom, and speak directly to the class. However, as had been well documented already in this book, 2020 was not the norm. The new process to handle this function was to host a Zoom meeting. Video conferencing was well entrenched into our everyday fabric by this time, so the Zoom concept was not unfamiliar to me. I explained that I was traveling on my next adventure to Egypt, and would be available to participate in the Zoom conference after I returned. Therefore, we established a meeting time to conduct the Q&A session, and record the meeting at the beginning of October, 2020.

No matter what medium was used for this speaking opportunity, this was a big moment for me. Definitely a first, and I wanted to make sure that I remained humble throughout the process. That might sound like an odd statement, but I had my reasons for feeling this way. You see, my book was one of two books that were assigned for the semester. Another person's book that was assigned was written by a lady, who I believe became the first woman on record to visit every country in the world. Certainly, a book that sounds like it was worth reading, and indeed I looked into purchasing it, because I am also an avid reader. I knew I would find interest in a fellow traveler's excepts. How shocked I was when I located the book on Amazon, and it carried a 65.00 price tag with it. Since that price was a bit too much for me, given this was just a standard hard back book, by someone who had become somewhat of a minor celebrity, I decided to pass on buying it. It came as no surprise to me when Roberta shared with me that this other author declined to speak with the class unless a rather high speaking fee was offered. I asked for no speaking fees, and was happy to have a chance to speak to a group of college students who were interested in my work.

When the Zoom interview started, it was in the form of some random
questions that dealt with my background in travel, my reasons for writing
the book, and a few areas of what my travel experiences had been, and
what were the memorable moments over the last 35 years. It didn't take
my long to feel quite comfortable in that format, and soon it felt like I
was just speaking with a longtime friend, catching them up on what I had
been doing through all these years. The old adage of "Time flies when
you are having fun" fit this situation, as I managed to ramble on for over
45 minutes, and didn't break a sweat. The one question that really stuck
with me was when Roberta asked me "what message did I want to convey
to the students". This did not take me very long to answer because it has
been something that I have been impressing upon to my own children
for many years. My answer was quite simple, "find your passion, and the
dollars will find you". Too many people, including myself many years ago,
think the answer to happiness lies is making money. A person needs to
make a certain level of income with which to sustain themselves, but if
your guiding light is to make more money, while doing it in an occupation
that you are not passionate about, your chances for long term satisfaction
are bleak. I believe that when you are passionate about something, your
true success will shine, and the money will follow, because you perform at
a higher level.

This is a philosophy that I have embraced for the last 10 years or so, after
falling for the corporate ladder trap of simply focusing on the base salary.
I remember thinking that I was never so unhappy, as when I made my
most amount of money. This principal may not hold true for every person
out there, but it is something I have tried to install in my daughters as
they entered into their young adult years. It has even been suggested
to me that On Top of The World is my legacy to pass on to my children. I
don't know if would call it a legacy, but it definitely falls under a category
of "lasting achievement", one that I am grateful to share with others.

8.

It's A Long Way to the Top

Coming into the last quarter of 2020, it had been a pretty busy year up to that point. Especially odd was most of that time, the narrative was that we were to stay home, shelter in place, "stay home, save lives", and all the rest of that propaganda garbage. I on the other hand was having none of that, and continued my own private battle to challenge the narrative. Still, it would have been easy for me to say, I have had a great year, but now I'm going to relax for the last 3 Months of 2020. Relaxing in the traditional style has never been what I am about, and in fact, I could argue that doing all of the adventurous pursuits I have done, is my form of relaxation. There will always be little adventures that one can do, but even I thought I didn't really have another grand adventure that would take place before the end of the year.

Over the last couple of years, I have learned that when the iron is hot, you need to strike, because you sometimes don't get that second chance. That is exactly what happened towards the end of 2020, and I made sure to seize a very unexpected opportunity. During my interview with Roberta Alison in October of 2020, one of the questions she asked me was "what was next". While I didn't know exactly what I was planning, I rattled off a couple of thoughts of things I still had in my proverbial bucket list. I have 3 main travel goals that I have been working in parallel, and have continued to build upon, sometimes accidentally. My number 1 goal has been to visit all 7 continents. With my recent trip to Egypt, I had reached number 6, with only a trip to Antarctica alluding my grasp of all 7 continents. A 2nd goal has been to visit all 50 states in this country, and I am happy to say, I am very close to achieving that. My 3rd goal is to be able to see the 7 Natural Wonders of the World. Having seen the Aurora Borealis in January of 2020, my umber had reached 5. The 2 wonders that were left on my list were Victoria Falls, located on the border of Zambia/Zimbabwe in Sub Saharan Africa, and a place called Volcan Paricutin, which was somewhere in Central Mexico.

My thought process at the time was that if somehow made it to Victoria

63

Falls, then I would have to go to Paricutin, just to complete that mission.
I really knew very little about Paricutin, other than it was a volcano
that erupted, and covered a city with lava. That is not the first time in
history that an event such as this has happened, as it would be almost
impossible to go through primary education without hearing the story
of the eruption of Mt. Vesuvius in Pompeii Italy. What makes Paricutin
so intriguing was that this eruption took place in 1943, when an existing
farm field opened from the center, and began spraying lava into the air.
The city of San Juan Paricutin was soon covered completely in lava. As I
continued to learn and research this phenomenon more, I learned where
exactly in Mexico it was, and just how easy it really was to get there.

Having discovered that the volcano was located in Central Mexico in
between Mexico City, and Guadalajara, near a town called Uruapan, I
started to get curious as to how I could travel there. When I researched
flights, my immediate go to airport for international flights is always LAX,
and this was no different. As I suspected, it was going to be an ordeal
to travel there with long connections in Mexican airports, or long land
journeys if I were to fly into large cities. My mental make-up usually has
me thinking that there "is always a better way", and that served me well
here. The area of Southern California that I live in is pretty convenient
when it comes to airports, as there a several major airports within a
100 miles radius from my home. After checking flights from the various
airports, and having very little success, I almost forgot the diamond in the
rough. The city of Tijuana, a large city in Mexico that borders the United
States near San Diego, has a large airport. Over the years, many people
have told me that they would fly from Tijuana, especially traveling within
Mexico, because the air fares were so much cheaper than in the U.S. I
had never flown out of this airport before, even though it is only about 90
miles from my house. Still, it was worth checking in to, and I am so glad I
did, because it made what I would call the **"Harvest Adventure"** a reality.

Harvest Adventure

I was able to find a very inexpensive flight from Tijuana on a Mexican
Low-cost carrier called Volaris, and I was even more surprised that they
offered nonstop service into the city of Uruapan. I was flying into the
city that was only about 20 miles from the volcano without any long

connection times and lost luggage. Suddenly, it was "game on" or in other words, time to climb a volcano, and see my 6th Natural Wonder of the World. I decided to travel the week of Thanksgiving, using company holiday time tied into vacation days as making for a longer trip. This was going to be a shorter trip than I normally take, but I only had one goal for this trip, which was to climb Volcan Paricutin.

All of the logistics were taken care of, plane tickets, hotels, and some local tours, so all I had to do was go. Right about the time leading up to the trip, the country moved back into a fear mongering stage regarding Covid. Fauci continued spewing his nonsense that families should not gather for holidays, and California's moronic Governor Gavin Newsome stated that people should not travel outside state lines. This silliness only fueled my desire to travel, and motivated me even more to stick it to the establishment. A week before I was scheduled to leave, the "no crossing state lines" proclamation was made, which prompted a friend to send me a message saying it looked like I wasn't going to be able to go. Sadly, I sensed a bit of joy in his tone, as if I would not have the final say. I would need to be physically stopped at the border in order for me not to take this trip.

Departure day was the Sunday before Thanksgiving, and an early morning drive from my home to the border near San Diego was underway. Normally the thought of having to cross a border, then go to an airport to fly sounded like a significant hassle. However, I had recently been told about the new Cross Border service that was opened in San Diego, for passengers flying from Tijuana. This service allows you to go through immigration while still in the United States, then walk across a bridge right into the Tijuana Airport terminal. I literally walked about 100 yards across an indoor bridge, and was in Mexico. This was one of the smoothest international transfers I had ever experienced, and the $30.00 service charge was well worth the investment.

Before I knew it, I was on the plane jetting to the city of Uruapan, in the state of Michoacán. I only had 3 full days with which to carry out my mission on this adventure, so there would be little down time. Arrival in Uruapan was uneventful, if not a little unnerving, as heavily armed guards were present at the airport. This part of Mexico is somewhat notorious for the drug cartel stories, and some of the violence that takes place. The truth is, that while yes, these things do happen, they can happen anywhere, and I think that many places in Mexico receive a lot of bad press about crime, drugs & safety. As my experience would show me, a lot of what I had heard was nothing more than sensational news stories.

My first day in Uruapan was about getting my barriers, and planning for the next day which is when I would climb Volcan Paricutin. I ventured around town just experiencing the local culture, and walked to the edge of the city where there was a beautiful National Park right in the middle of everything. A quiet refuge filled with waterfalls and walking trails, was a huge break from the hustle and bustle of the second largest city of Michoacán. After spending a couple of hours within the park, I took a nice walk back through the streets of Uruapan, and made plenty of time to enjoy a few Corona beers, as the strength of the US dollar had the exchange rate at about .75 cents per beer. Since Mexico was still in the heavy throws of Covid, tourism was still low, and prices for just about everything were extremely low. Food, drink, hotel rooms, souvenirs, all were available at rock bottom prices. A late afternoon walk to the main bus station to purchase a ticket for a trip to the city of Morelia on day 3, rounded out my first day. The only thing left was an evening on the town for dinner, mariachi music and of course .75 cent beers, which was the perfect way to end day 1. Tomorrow would be a full day of adventure and history, and I wanted to make sure I was well rested for it.

Volcan Paricutin

My original intention was to hike Paricutin like a local using independent means, and local transportation services to get there. However, because of Covid, many of the services were closed, or went out of business altogether. This meant I needed to arrange a private tour to get to the volcano, and in reality, it turned out to be a good idea. The drive took about an hour, and it was just myself, and my guide, who would be with me the whole day. The tour was really divided into two parts, with the first being the actual climb of the volcano. The second would be a visit to the ruins of the city of San Juan Paricutin, which was almost 100% covered in lava when the volcano erupted in 1943. We were able to drive up until about a quarter mile away from the base of the volcano. The rest of the way would be on foot walking over lava rock and ash, and within about 15 minutes, I stood before the base of a Natural Wonder of the World. I had made it, but this was only the beginning of the adventure.

There are 2 paths that one can take when climbing the volcano. There is a direct path, which is a much steeper grade, but takes considerably less time to reach the crater at the top. The 2nd path takes a much longer approach, with a significantly less grade, which is probably the one most people choose to take. My guide explained both of the paths to me, and then informed me that he would not be climbing with me. I also got the feeling that he would have preferred I take the shorter route, so he would not have to wait as long, since I was his only guest hiking that day. I pondered the choice for about a minute or so, and then decided to take the short, steep route, fueled by a little of my own arrogance, that I can still do anything at 56 years old. This was decision that I would come to regret in a short period of time.

I grabbed a long staff to help with balance and support, and started my ascent. The surface of the volcano is 100% ash, and made the climbing incredibly difficult. Picture yourself climbing a hill at the beach, as every step your feet sink at least 6 inches or more into the ash. At first, I was motivated by adrenaline and pushed hard, but soon I found myself taking frequent breaks, only to look back and see I hadn't really gone very far. I pushed and pushed as I was determined not to fail at this adventure, and then it hit. One thing I did not give much thought to was the altitude at which Paricutin sits. The summit is a little over 10,000 feet, which by most standards is pretty high, however, I have been at higher elevations without any issues before. My trip to Everest in 2017, had me standing at 17,000 feet, and never once did I experience any issues.

As I pushed to just under 10,000 feet, I felt the dizziness coming on. This was exactly the same feeling I had when I was hiking the Great Wall of China, where I became so fatigued that I was overwhelmed by dizziness, and I had to lay down for about 10 minutes before it subsided. During that hike, a lady that was part of the tour had given me some chocolate, and after having that, and resting those 10 minutes, I was able to continue on with the hike. This time I was prepared for this event, and had a supply of chocolate in my back pack. I found myself laying on the side of an ash covered volcano, at 10,000 feet eating a chocolate bar, all the while hoping the dizziness would dissipate.

What made this experience a little more stressful was that there was no one else hiking on the volcano. I was the only person hiking this thing, and my guide was way at the bottom, unable to assist me in anyway, if I were to find myself in distress. I gave it about 15 minutes, laying in the ash, sun shining, and not a soul to be seen, before I aborted my climb. I felt a little better, but there was still some dizziness, and I was about ¼ of the way from the top. There may have been a time in my life, where I would have said "screw it", and pushed myself to the top. Had I done that, and became in even more distress, there would have been no one to help me. Through this whole Mid Life Adventure phase of my life, I have been guided by the motto of "grow your limits, but know your limits"

The decision to abort was not an easy thing for me, and as I slid down the ash on my backside, I did have a feeling of disappointment. A climb that took 45 minutes to ascend, was over with about a 3-minute slide back down, without realizing my goal to look within the crater of this volcano. The disappointment didn't last long, because I realized what I had done, was already more than I ever thought I could achieve, and I would live to climb more mountains, and possibly an even more famous volcano in the future.

Having returned to a respectable altitude, and feeling much better as the dizziness at the lower level subsided, my guide took me to the ruins of San Juan Paricutin. This entire city was covered in lava, except for a few elements of the church, which are still uncovered. The main facade of the church is still visible, along with parts of the sanctuary, that many people return to on a regular basis to lay flowers, and other remembrances. I found it amazing at how course the lava rock really was, and that one slip, could seriously cut into one's flesh, like a razor-sharp knife. This was history that I was standing on, and not the history of hundreds or thousands of years ago, but history that was made just 70 years ago. I left Paricutin with one more Natural Wonder of the World under my belt, and while I fell short on one of my goals, seeing this wonder was every bit the adventure I thought it would be.

My final day in Mexico could have easily been spent kicking around the streets of Uruapan in a relaxing mode, but I am always about doing the most with the least, and this trip wasn't going to change that. The capital city of Michoacán is Morelia, and it was only a 90-minute bus ride from Uruapan, so off we went bright and early on day 3. I found a local guided city tour, and booked that with a guide named Rodrigo, from Yei Tours. As been so often the case during Covid trips, it was just me on this city tour, so in essence, this was a private tour. Rodrigo took me around the city, explaining the history, taking me inside the many churches, and showing me the rich tradition of Spanish architecture. Because Morelia is the largest city in this state, it didn't take long for me to spot the local Wal Mart and Home Depot along the way. After spending about 6 hours with Rodrigo, I mentioned that I still needed to pick up a few souvenirs for this trip. He took me to a local museum, where all the work was done by local artists, and therefore, all the profits went back into the local economy. Certainly, a great a cause to support, and I found some cool memorabilia to purchase. That is when some drama kicked in when I went to pay for my items, and discovered that my ATM card was missing! A quick run through the rolodex of my mind had me remembering that I withdrew money at an ATM in Uruapan the day before, and forgot to grab my card from the machine. A panicked call with a 10-minute hold time to my bank ensued, until I was able to cancel the card, and have a new one sent to my home. Fortunately, the card had not been compromised, and all funds intact, so a big sigh of relief was had by me.

Soon it was time for me to head back to Uruapan, so that I would be able to catch my flight back to Tijuana later that evening. The flight home was smooth, clearing immigration at the airport was just as fluid, and soon I was back in the United States driving home from San Diego. I had expected the traffic to be crazy as it usually is on the day before Thanksgiving, but to my surprise, traffic was relatively light. I had a turkey to prep for dinner the next day, as my daughters would be joining me to celebrate the Holiday. Having the chance to make this impromptu trip is the very definition of adventure travel. Facing another climb in the mountain of life, seeing my 6th Natural Wonder of the World, and defying the mainstream narrative that we must stay home to save lives, made the trip that much more memorable. A big shout out to Gavin Newsome, and all the rest of his ilk, for inspiring the motto "they told me I couldn't, so I did".

Climbing Volcan Paricutin
Uruapan, MX. November, 2020

Exploring the ruins of San Juan Paricutin
Uruapan, MX. November, 2020

9.

Mmm Mmm Mmm Mmm

Having two major adventures within a relatively short period of time had me thinking it was time to take a little break from the traveling, or at least the major traveling. It also had me thinking it was time to address a health-related issue that had been bothering me for the better part of 2020. While the world wrestled with the fears of Covid, I was experiencing a problem with significant pain in my right shoulder. I finally decided to seek medical help in late September, and after a couple of MRIs, it was confirmed that I had an impingement issue, and possible rotator cuff problem. The doctor advised that I could treat it conservatively with medication and rest, or aggressively with surgery. Having gone through this problem on my left shoulder back in 2005, and ultimately having surgery when the conservative measures did not work, I chose the surgery option right away. Because of the Harvest Adventure trip, I had planned in late November, I opted to have the surgery scheduled for mid-December. It might leave you wondering why I would have a surgery scheduled so close to the Christmas holiday, but it was a pretty logical choice. Like so many other decisions in life, this came down to a financial decision. Since I had met my out-of-pocket maximum for the year, I could have the surgery in December at no cost to me, or wait till January and pay $4,000.00 of my own money.

So, I finished 2020 with a small adventure that I referred to as "Self on the Shelf", which I borrowed from the holiday elf concept, realizing I would be somewhat out of commission for a few months. The surgery went well, and there was no tear to the rotator cuff, but I did have some bone shaved off and removed, but the prognosis was better than originally thought. During my recovery, I had time to plot out my next adventure. I rather foolishly thought I could recover in about 2 months, and would be back on the slopes for at least 1 time before the 2021 ski season would end. Knowing I wasn't going to get a true ski trip in, I decided I wanted to do something a little lower key, but still perhaps something that was new for me. A few weeks into January, I needed to meet with one of my customers in the Salt Lake area. I worked the meeting so that I could take the week end, and roam about the Rocky Mountains. If I couldn't ski, I could at least enjoy a few days of Winter in the mountains. This played into another of my bucket list items, and would let me check off another thing I wanted to do.

Visiting all 50 states is goal that I have come very close to achieving, and the only states that remained on this list are the ones I refer to as the 3 M's. Maine, Mississippi, and Montana are the last 3 states I need to visit in order to reach this particular goal. Since I would already be in Salt Lake for business, it was time for me to drive a few hours North, and cross the border into my 48th state of Montana. I would only have the week end with which to experience this, and I was still somewhat limited with my mobility, but I managed to turn this trip into what I would call the **"Big Sky Adventure"**.

I had never been to Yellowstone National Park before, and the Winter time is definitely not the best time to visit. Most of the park is closed for the Winter Season, but there is a small part of the park that is open year-round, and West Yellowstone happened to be the closest to where I was driving from. The plan was for me to meet with a client near Utah State University in Logan Utah, then from there, I would start my journey North through Idaho, and into Montana.

I had always wanted to see Montana, and have been told by many people that it is filled with beautiful scenery, and I was finally going to witness this for myself. Living in California for over 35 years, dealing with huge populations is something you have to deal with, but also leaves the mind wondering as to what it would be like to live somewhere, without all the crowds. The rough estimates of population for California hover around 40-45 million people in the state. Montana has an estimated population of barely over 1 million people. I was about to find out what it meant when people said there is a lot of land in Montana.

As I was driving North through the Idaho basin, the snow in the mountains on both sides of the highway was stunning. Driving through small towns such as Pocatello and Idaho Falls left me thinking "could I truly see myself living in a town of only 50,000 people", or would I need more than a town that size could offer. As I continued, the depth level and coverage of snow became greater. There was no shortage of snow in this area, unlike what Salt Lake had been experiencing. Stopping at rest area for some coffee and gas, I took a 360 degree look around, and saw nothing but snow-covered mountains. My inner peace has always been brought to the surface when I am in the presence of quiet mountains playing host to snow. Certainly, a nice respite from the everyday hustle & bustle of the city. Another 30 minutes, and my new goal was achieved as I could see in the distance what had alluded me for a long time, the sign that said "Welcome to Montana". Of course, I had to pull over to the side of the road, walk through 2-foot snow drifts, just so I could take the inevitable selfie of me in front of the sign. State number 48 was in the books, now I just had to find something fun to do.

My final destination for this day was Bozeman Montana. Not really sure why I chose Bozeman, other than it was probably the largest small city I could find, that was within reasonable driving distance. With just about 47,000 people, Bozeman is not quite the size of Missoula, or Billings, but still large enough to offer some amenities that I am normally used to. If I ever had a scenario where I placed a location on a dart board, threw a dart, and said, that is where I am going, this was probably close to that. I had a chance to go into the town for dinner, and found that Bozeman is very much a town with the Old West flavor. Missoula is much more of a college town, and a little hipper, while Bozeman has that small-town, laid-back cowboy feel. Given that many places were still observing Covid protocols, finding a place for dinner, or an old-style saloon, proved to be a bit problematic. I was able to find a place that had craft beer, and pub food, but they closed at 9pm on a Friday night, so rather than enjoy my time, and take in the local atmosphere, I had to rush through my meal. I finished up the evening walking the streets in town, and was pleased to see that much of the holiday lights were still in place, even though we were well into the second week of January.

The next morning, I was up early and out of my hotel, for today I would head back South and drive through parts of Yellowstone National Park. There is something to be said for driving on an interstate with no posted speed limit, Sirius XM set to First Wave, and nothing but mountains covered in snow. Unless of course it is driving through a snow-covered Yellowstone National Park. I can only imagine what the entire park is like to drive through, but if this small part is any indication, this will be something that I must return to, at the proper time of the year. On the way back to West Yellowstone, I passed one of the most famous ski resorts in Montana, Big Sky. I thought about deviating and driving up to see the resort closer, but me fresh out of a sling, and unable to really do anything, chose to by-pass that, and save myself the disappointment of a lost ski season.

I pulled back into West Yellowstone in the late morning, and was ahead of my travel schedule. I still had to be back in Salt Lake later tonight for the flight back home, but now I had some extra time to spend in this small resort town. I had read about a grizzly bear sanctuary in the area, and knew I had some time to check it out. I'll admit I have a strong admiration for nature, and the animals that roam it. It is always such a delicate balance of man and nature, and it often saddens me that nature will often lose out to the needs of man. Nonetheless, I really wanted my chance to see some actual grizzlies, so I checked out the Grizzly & Wolf Discovery Center. This was a small habitat that not only housed some grizzly bears, but also served as a wolf sanctuary. Since I was documenting this trip for my YouTube channel, I did some filming of both the wolves and grizzlies, along with my documentary footage.

The overall experience was a bit disappointing in that it was a relatively small area, and they had only 2 bears visible at a given time. I discovered that it really was a tourist trap for the admission price, and the value of what was offered, but I did get to see another first, the American grizzly bear. Of course, no trip to a tourist trap is complete without the obligatory exit through the gift shop. I probably would have done better to choose a sanctuary that I drove past in the Bozeman area, but thought Yellowstone, might be the better option.

Before pulling out of West Yellowstone, I needed to fill up the tank, grab a large coffee, and oddly enough, I had to purchase a bottle of windshield washer fluid as the car ran out of fluid to clean the windshield. Soon I was back on the road traversing the plateau of Idaho again as I continued to head South towards Salt Lake. I entered the Salt Lake valley just in time to catch an amazing sunset that was an incredible fire orange color. It was right about this time that I realized that the washer fluid in the car was not empty, but somehow must have frozen up, as I went to add in more fluid, only to find the fluid level was completely filled. That turned out to be a $3.50 investment that I will never get back, but it was the conclusion to a really quick, but exciting small adventure. As I flew home that night, I took a moment to re-cap another completed journey, and the realization to one of my parallel goals, as now my 50-state goal was down to the 2 M's. Maine & Mississippi are now on the clock.

The beauty of Yellowstone National Park in Winter
Montana. January, 2021

Big Sky Mountain
West Yellowstone, Montana. January, 2021

10.

The Great Gig in the Sky

Now that 2021 was underway, things had to get better right? I mean, after a solid year, all this pandemic nonsense had to end right? My early appraisal of the situation turned out to be more optimistic than even I could have known. For almost 1 solid year, I battled the narrative, defied the odds, and proved that you didn't have to live in fear. I guess I had secretly hoped that my message would resonate with others, and I wouldn't be the only maverick out there. As I returned from my Big Sky Adventure, I saw no indication that things were going to return to at least a somewhat normal lifestyle I was used to, which only doubled my resolve. That meant that 2021 had to be an even more adventurous year than 2020 was. A tall order, seeing as how I made 3 epic trips in 2020, and two of those were international.

I also had to deal with the reality that adventures cost money, and yes, even with a few business travel perks, the costs can add still add up. The factual element I was faced with is the salary reduction that I had to absorb a year earlier was still in place, and was still very much a part of everyday life. I was able to cut back in 2020, and adjust a few luxuries that I allowed myself previously, all in the name of traveling. If I wanted to continue that, something would have to make up for the shortfall. It's not that I was opposed to taking a second job, but more an issue of the travel requirements of my primary role. Under normal circumstances, I could often travel 2 or even 3 times per month, depending upon the need. That uncertainty, precluded me from having any type of regular secondary income. If I could find something that allowed me the flexibility to work when I could/wanted, I would be more than willing to put the time in.

One thing the pandemic did was bring to the forefront, the "Gig" economy. A variety of delivery services, that allowed many people to stay home (save lives), and have others deliver goods & services. My daughter had latched on to a grocery delivery service called Instacart, and suggested I give it try. She had done pretty well using it to supplement her income, as her other job was part time. At first, I somewhat

77

balked at the idea, I mean how would that look as a 57-year-old man delivering groceries. But if I wanted to continue my life style, and enjoy my adventures, vanity had to take a backseat to pragmatism. I signed up online and within a few days, I had all the credentials to start this new adventure. It took me a couple of days to get the hang of using the app, and learning some of the local stores, but I started to get more comfortable, and was on my way. I had found something that allowed me to work nights and week end hours, when I wanted to, and accepting orders that I wanted to.

I'll admit I was blown away after my first week when I made a little over $500.00 for about 15 total hours of work. I worked hard, and like I always try to do in any job, I wanted to be as diligent as possible. It wasn't without its drawbacks, as I accepted some orders that were not worth what they were paying, but I was building the knowledge where I would soon be working smarter, not harder. It wasn't long before I had created my own system for maximizing profits, and limiting the types of stores I would accept orders for. One of the hardest things about doing this type of work was not knowing the layout of the store, which probably doubled the amount of time needed to actually complete the task. It wasn't long before I narrowed down the number of stores where I was willing to work, which ones had the best paying orders, and the ones I became the most familiar with. It also wasn't long before I started to spend the extra money I was making on things that I needed, ok, wanted! Since I had mapped out a Spring adventure already, I started focusing on things that I would need for that trip. One area I was upgrading was my photography equipment, and for anyone familiar with photography, it is not an inexpensive hobby. I bought a few things for my camera, mostly around zoom lenses, which was something I knew would enhance the quality of the pictures, and video I would be taking on this next trip.

What I found out was that your life can very easily become accustomed to things when you have extra money coming in. The high of feeling that quick cash come in on a weekly, or even daily basis, can be so addicting. There were times when I would go and buy something, with the notion that I'll just work a week of delivering groceries, and it will be paid off. I suppose that is a better alternative than buying something on a credit card, and paying it off slowly, along with accruing interest. The more I

made, the more I saved, and spent, and before I knew it, the upcoming
trip was paid off, and all the little extras I wanted to have for it, were
in place. It got to the point where the first 5 months of 2021, my focus
became my regular job, my part time job, and my walking regimen. There
was little time for much else, and that was OK with me.

My short-term goal for this part time "gig", was to earn enough money to
cover the cost of my adventure, get a few toys along the way, and then
be done with it. That's not exactly how things worked out, because as
I would find out, this part time work was actually a social outlet for me
too. The extra work filled the space of a lot of dead time that I had, and
in fact I could make the case that it had a lot to do with my writing hiatus.
The extra money was good, the time commitment was relatively minimal,
and it kept this single guy busy, instead of wasting time with TV, or some
other means of killing time. Still, I was always mindful that this new found
money maker could at any time dry up. These "gig" economy jobs are
definitely a niche play, and you should never rely on something like this
as your main source of income. Still, my plan was to return to my normal
lifestyle after I returned from my Spring adventure, and I would have no
problem leaving this extracurricular activity behind.

Or would I?

11.

Circle of Life

I have often been asked how I decide what adventures I am going to take
and when. It's not always an easy answer, and there are many factors
that weigh into a decision of where to travel too next. I do have some
goals, and the interest that aligns with those goals, but as I have said
many times before, circumstances sometimes dictate where my next
trip ends up being. At the beginning of 2021, I wanted to change things
up a bit from what had become a routine. Over the last several years, I
would schedule my big adventures during the month of September. There
were usually a couple of reasons for my thinking, but the 2 big reasons
are usually, low season, and still favorable weather. My previous trips to
China, Russia and Egypt were all done in September, where the heavy
crowds had waned, and the weather was still decent.

I started thinking about taking a Spring adventure, and that could possibly
allow me to fit 2 adventures into the year. I had done 2 adventures in
2020, but nothing about 2020 was normal, and I thought how the last half
of that year played out, was more of a fluke. This year I would map out
a strategy to have 2 big adventures, one for the Spring and perhaps one
for Fall. I had been thinking for a while about taking a trip over one of the
major holiday time frames, and this year seemed like I could make that
happen. Now that I had the time frames mapped out, all I needed to do
was choose a place to go. Kind of a backwards approach I know, but this is
often how I roll.

There were many elements of the pandemic that were really negative,
but one of the things that was a positive for me, was inexpensive travel
prices, particularly when it came to air fare. I know it sounds kind of
selfish on my part, but I really enjoyed traveling during the pandemic,
because I was often bumped into first class, and I found some ridiculously
cheap air fares to international destinations. When I started to plan where
I wanted to go, it was almost like the dart board concept, where I would
pick a place that I was interested in, then do an air fare search. Like all of
my trips seem to be, a lot of challenges and detailed planning require a

significant time investment, which is actually part of the fun.

The Spring trip started with me coming across a crazy inexpensive price to Spain. I had never been there before, so it would be a first for me, but I had another motive. Spain was a place that my daughter Megan had said she would like to go to, since she had never been to Europe. So, when I came across a $550.00 round trip fare during the summer months, I was ready to pounce. I called Megan, and asked if she would like to go to Spain with me on an adventure. I was surprised, because when you find these deals, you have to jump on them right away. Her response was "can I let you know tomorrow". I said "sure, but don't wait too long". I already had mapped out a strategy to schedule this trip so I could be in Pamplona to "run with the bulls". That is my kind of adventure, along with the other sightseeing elements that Spain would have to offer. The next day, Megan called me and said "Let's do it dad". Sadly, when I went to book the tickets, the price had changed to $1100.00 roundtrip for the exact same dates. In 24 hours, the price went from crazy cheap, to same ole same ole. With the new price in play, Megan was out, and I was back to the drawing board.

Starting a new destination search was a bit deflating in that I had 24 hours to get excited about a potential trip to Spain with my daughter, that now wasn't going to happen. I sat down at the computer and essentially played my proverbial dart game, and started picking places I was interested in. I looked into Thailand, then some potential spots in Europe, mostly Greece, as the prices to Athens were really pretty good. Then I plugged in a search of Nairobi, and was shocked at what came back. I had no inkling of traveling back to Africa so quickly, after having just returned from there less than 4 months earlier. I figured I had met my goal of touching Africa as my 6th continent, so I would turn my focus to somewhere else. But a roundtrip ticket to Kenya for only $660.00 was something that I found impossible to ignore. I have always had the idea of doing some version of a safari on my to do list, just wasn't sure when it would come about. As it turns out, it was now going to be in May of 2021.

I pulled the trigger on the airline ticket, and now it was time to plan the adventure. I knew I wanted to do an escorted safari, but I soon found out that there was a wide variation of the types of safaris that you can take.

One can take a budget safari, or one can spend a whole lot of money on a lavish safari. For me it was all about the adventure, and having WIFI in a tent, and many other plush amenities wasn't a priority. I opted for the more modest setup staying in private tents, but still retaining the "roughing it" feel. Since I was going that far, I couldn't just stay in Kenya, I had to add more and make this an even greater adventure. That led to an expansion of my trip to the country of Zambia, which is where I would witness the last item of my quest to see the 7 Natural Wonders of the World, when my eyes would bestow upon Victoria Falls. I was about to complete on of the keystone pieces of my world travels, having seen all 7. This adventure was going to be epic, and nothing was going to change that, or so I told myself.

Traveling to Sub Saharan Africa was a new thing for me, and I would soon learn just how much is required to engage a trip of this magnitude, long before you leave. I would discover the plethora of shots and vaccines that were required for me to travel into this area, let alone the heighted emotion surrounding the Covid vaccine, and the propagandist push for Americans to get it. I knew I had to have booster shots on some immunizations that I had previously, but I also needed to get a Yellow Fever vaccine. With all of this swirling about, I thought about the Covid vaccine as well. I am not an anti-vax person, nor did I feel I was more vulnerable if I chose not to get it. By this time, many people had already received the vaccine, and there were some stories of adverse reactions, but it seemed relatively safe. I also didn't buy into the conspiracy theories about micro-chips etc., hidden inside. So, what to do?

Whenever I travel, I always want the least number of complications possible when traveling between countries, crossing borders etc., so I hedged my bet. I gambled that if I got the Covid vaccine, most countries would by-pass the need for negative Covid tests to enter the country. Having to find a testing center overseas, sounded like more of a hassle to me, so I decided to get the vaccine, and hoped those nuisances would go away. My gamble failed as I still had to provide negative tests for each country I entered. This trip was going to require 3 separate tests, in order to avoid any delays. I also had to be mindful that I was traveling to the Southern Hemisphere, and therefore traveling in the May/June time frame, would actually be late Fall, early Winter where I was going.

Armed with a whole lot of new camera and video equipment, I headed to LAX on May 21st, 2021 for the African Adventure. First stop was the 10-hour flight to Amsterdam, then followed by another 8-hour flight into Nairobi. I would soon learn just how massive the continent of Africa really was. The flight over was pretty uneventful as I learned on my previous trip to Russia, that KLM is not the respected airline it used to be many years ago. They clearly have become a middle of the pack player. I arrived safely along with my bags, so that truly is a win in my book. A very late arrival into Nairobi, and a ride to the hotel had me exhausted, but since I built in a rest day before the start of the safari, I knew I was able to catch up on any rest I needed. I had one day to spend in Nairobi, and I used that day to collect some elements I was going to need since I would be off the grid for the better part of 6 days. Bug spray, tooth paste snacks and a few other things were stocked up on, and a little wandering around a small part of the city was how I spent my day. I took notice that most of the hotels had guards and gates at the entrance, and I started to get the feel that if you were not a guest at the hotel, you were not especially welcome at the property. A theme I would notice throughout most of the country of the next 7 days.

I woke up early the next morning and was all set to experience the Circle of Life. Nairobi itself seemed just like a big capital city, but I would soon be out in the bush that would have me seeing the most magnificent game animals in their natural habitat. My safari guide James, arrived at the hotel to pick me up, and has been the case through this entire pandemic, my 7-person safari, turned out to be only me. I was now a safari of one, a completely private safari if you will. This may sound ideal to many people, but considering I travel alone, one of the best chances I have to actually meet other people is when I take tours such as this. In that respect, it was a little disappointing to be on my own. A 3-hour drive later through the Great Rift Valley, James had me at Lake Nakuru National Park for an afternoon game drive. This park boasts the ability to see the Big 5, but seeing lions in this park is a rarity. I did see tons of zebras, cape buffaloes, plenty of giraffes, a few rhinos, and we even spotted an elusive leopard. The leopard is believed to be the toughest of the Big 5 to spot, as they are quite timid, and blend in with the scenery so well. I wasn't able to snap a picture of the one we saw, but I did get to see him slinking in the grasslands. After a few hours in the park, it was back to the small hotel for an overnight stay, and an early departure the next day. Day 2 would be the cornerstone of the safari, because for the next 2 days we would be visiting what arguably is one of the best game reserve parks in Kenya, if not all of Africa, the Masai Mara.

The Masai Mara is the largest game reserve in Kenya located in the Southwestern part of Kenya, that borders the country of Tanzania. It was in this famous reserve where I would have the most likely chance of seeing the animals, that previously had been reserved for me to see on NATGEO TV. We had 2 days of Game drives in this park, and I wasn't sure if that was going to be enough. James had us in the park on day one in the late afternoon, about 2 hours before the sun would set. More cape buffaloes, gazelles, and a whole lot of wildebeests made themselves available for pictures and video. Further into the park we went, and more animals were just grazing along. We would come across a small pack of cheetah's sleeping in the afternoon sun, and the occasional wart hog. I saw Pumba, and quickly learned that they are extremely scared animals. Every Pumba I tried to photograph would run away, as if they knew what I was trying to do. Of course, being one of the top delicacies for apex predators, I can understand their nervousness. As we headed out towards the entrance of the park, James stopped and allowed me to photograph an amazing sunset over the Masai Mara. Taking in those few moments and photographing the sunset on the Mara, was another moment where I felt blessed, taking stock of what my eyes have seen. If the first day in the Mara wasn't enough, I had another full day tomorrow that would hold the last links to my Big 5 quest.

An early start to the 2nd day in the Mara was the order of the day, as was a "no hot water" shower in my tented camp. Making the best of these little inconveniences is to be expected, but I will admit that a cold shower is my least favorite way to start a day. The camp packed us a lunch as this would be a full day inside the park. A day that would have us go all the way to the Tanzanian border with Kenya, for a visit to the Mara River. This area is famous for the Great Wildebeest Migration that occurs every year. We were driving through the park on a rather cool morning as this was the time of the year entering Kenya's Winter Season. The sun was out, and it was a quiet day so far with few animal sightings. Then out of nowhere, James makes a sharp right turn causing me to fly out of my seat. He pointed to an area way on the other side of the plateau, and said "I think I see lions". I couldn't see a damn thing, other than grass and a few trees, but he insisted there were lions there. He started driving around the roads to head in that direction, often creating a few new roads as we moved along. Since much of this was off the beaten path, it was quite bumpy, which is not the best environment for photography. He swung up around a giant set of rocks, when low and behold, we stumbled right into a pride of lions basking in the sun on a huge rock. Right out of The Lion King, this was my Pride Rock. There must have been 12 – 15 lions laying on this rock, sunning themselves, some sitting, many laying down, and a couple on the watch for food.

Word of the sighting soon spread to other guides, and before we knew there were 5 more safari trucks at the rock to see the lions. They remained unmoved by the sudden human interest, and in fact were perfect photography participants, as they went about their business, as if we were not there. They looked so docile, almost as if you could walk up and pet them, but no one was interested in testing that theory. I could not believe my eyes as I was no more than 25 feet away from them, observing them in their own habitat, and often having a lack of adjectives to describe what I was witnessing. We probably spent about 20 minutes watching, mostly to see if there would be any sort of attack on prey that wondered into the area. No such luck however, and soon it was time to continue on. There was only 1 missing piece to the Big 5, and it would not take long for us to check that box off.

Continuing to head towards the Mara River, we suddenly found ourselves surround by African Elephants on both sides of the road. Again, just going about their daily routines, it was amazing as elephants will continue moving in groups and do not fear visitors either as several walked within 10 feet of the vehicle. After a couple more hours driving, we arrived at the Mara River, which sits as a border between Kenya and Tanzania. On one side of the river, sits the Masai Mara Reserve, while on the other side of the river sits Serengeti National Park in Tanzania. In the middle of the river sits a huge number of Hippos, being closely monitored by crocodiles. It was incredible to watch those 2 animals respect each other's territory, and occasionally antagonize the other. As we started to head back, James stopped at the monument that identifies the border of Kenya & Tanzania.

As I walked about 100 feet to the south, I technically crossed into the country of Tanzania, though no official border crossing exists here, and the only true way to enter the country would have been to cross a crocodile infested river. No thank you!

The final stop on my week-long safari was a trip to Amboseli National Park. I decided to include this trip, not because of the animals, but because I would be able to view Mt. Kilimanjaro, from inside the park. Amboseli is again on the border of Tanzania, and Kilimanjaro sits on the Eastern end of Tanzania. To get there involved another long drive and a couple more nights in tented camps. The next morning, I woke up, and outside my cabin in the distance was the snow covered peak of Kilimanjaro, just like all the pictures I had ever seen. Being the highest peak in Africa, it was without a doubt worth the extra trip to see it. Finishing up the day in Amboseli was fairly uneventful as I saw tons of zebras, elephants, even a few hyenas. I learned the hyena is the 2nd apex predator in Africa, only behind the lion. They are a bit skittish when by themselves, preferring to attack in packs.

Unlucky 7

At the end of the safari, I arrived back into Nairobi, and back on the grid. I said good bye to James, thanked him, and gave him an extra-large tip. He provided me with a great experience, and I know he lost out on a lot of tip money with me being the only person on the tour. I was also looking forward to my first real shower and comfortable bed in 6 days, as I booked a Sheraton hotel at Nairobi airport. I also had a Covid test appointment at the local clinic there, that would allow me to continue on with my trip. It was at that point, being back on the grid, that a major setback was about to hit me, and leave me to make a very difficult decision.

It wasn't long being back in a communication zone that I started receiving travel updates, and one of the first ones I received, was not good. I had an update from Kenya Airways that a portion of my flight was canceled. The next day I was scheduled to fly from Nairobi to Livingstone, Zambia, spend 2 days in that area, then fly from Livingstone on to Cape Town South Africa for an additional 2 days. Well Kenya Airways canceled the

Livingstone to Cape Town portion of the trip. On the surface that might not seem to be a big deal, however, in this part of the world, when a flight cancels, there isn't another one leaving in 2 hours. In fact, the next flight was 6 days later. So, in essence, I would have been stuck in Zambia for 6 days, which wasn't going to work because I was leaving Nairobi to fly home in 5 days.

My only choice was to fly directly to Cape Town and by pass my stop in Zambia. This was a much greater deviation than just a late flight, or missed tour, as a significant piece of my trip was now being left out. An opportunity to see my last of the 7 Natural Wonders of the World had been whisked away because of a canceled flight. My planned bungee jump (a first) off the Zambezi bridge over Victoria Falls would not happen. Something that I had been planning for months, and had paid for in advance, now had to be changed, rearranged, and adjusted to fit a new schedule, all at the last minute, without any time to create a new plan. I had to act fast, and after I passed my Covid test, I had to make new arrangements for a trip to South Africa. I was now spending 4 days in Cape Town when originally, I was only spending 2. This meant I had to adjust my hotel accommodations, if I even could, arrange for airport transportation, and try to find other sightseeing adventures for 2 additional days.

In a cruel twist of irony, when I departed Nairobi, my flight to Cape Town stopped in Livingstone to let off passengers, and pick up passengers flying to Cape Town. I remember desperately trying to adjust my window seat as we started to land and flew on the left side of Victoria Falls. Taking pictures from an airplane window, at about 2500 feet wasn't going to cut, but I did the best I could. I could see the mist from the falls rising up in the distance, which only tormented me further. The nickname for Victoria Falls is "The smoke that thunders", and the harsh reality was that I would neither see the smoke, or hear the thunder up close because of this setback. I can view this event in one of two ways, in that I will be stuck on seeing 6 of the 7 Natural Wonders of the World, or I can say I have seen all 7 of them, with an asterisk (*) next to that claim. Either way, this event would shape my overall view of the trip, and became a prelude for what I could expect from Kenya Airways in the future.

Afrikaans

South Africa has long been a country on my radar to visit at some point in my journey of life. Like many countries, South Africa has had its own share of turmoil and struggles with independence post World War II. It also happens to be one of the most economically developed countries of Africa, and currently ranks 2nd in wealthiest countries within Africa, trailing only the Petroleum rich Nigeria. When I initially considered including South Africa on this trip, I reached out to a former colleague Gillian Huntoon, who is a native South African, to obtain some local expertise on a place I had never been to before. So, even though the circumstances of the changes in my trip had me very disappointed, I was very excited to head to a more Western driven country, after spending a week in the more primitive and tribal country of Kenya. The new plan was to spend 4 days in the city of Cape Town, in the western most part of the country. I was on my way to the Southernmost tip of the African continent, to a city that has been recently voted the number 1 city in all of Africa. Johannesburg, which is the largest city in South Africa, often gets the recognition because it is home to many international corporations, but the overall beauty, climate, and diversity of Cape Town. make it the favorite place to visit in South Africa.

When I arrived, I fully expected the modern amenities, but even I was surprised at the level of the infrastructure, and development in place. The ride in from the airport was no different than if I had arrived into New York or Los Angeles. Cape Town, like any other major city has areas that are completely safe, and areas that are extremely dangerous. My Uber driver dropped me off at my Hotel in the Waterfront area, the Beautiful Victoria & Alfred Hotel. Located close to everything in the Waterfront, this hotel was an amazing property, and was had for the very modest price of $80.00 per night. After check-in, I walked around the area to find an amazing array of shops, restaurants, bars, and a huge high end shopping mall right there. Like many cities these days, Cape Town has their own giant Ferris Wheel, that overlooks the entire harbor. After my long travel day, and getting a bit acclimated, it was time for dinner, and since I was by the water, fish & chips was calling, along with a local beer. Covid fear was still running pretty high, so to avoid all the mask craziness, I decided to eat outside, and take a break from all the hustle & bustle. The next 4 days would be very busy, as I had some element of adventure planned for each day, which also included time for a Covid test that would allow me to return home.

My 1st day of sights was a full day trip to the Cape Peninsula. We would visit several of the beach areas of Cape Town, including the famous Boulder Beach Penguin colony, home to thousands of African Penguins. As a rare treat, I would not be taking this tour solo, as 2 other guests were part of the group. A young lady from Guinea Bissau, and a college student studying in South Africa would join me for the day. We would then head to Cape Point, which would include a stop at the Cape of Good Hope, (The Southwestern most point of the African continent), and a hike to the Cape Lighthouse. The weather had been on again, off again with a mixture of sun and rain. This was Winter in this region, and the further South you go, the colder it is. We were as far South as you could possibly go in Africa, so in addition to the rain, the temperature was cool as well. I managed to get my picture in front of the Cape of Good Hope sign, along with my Steeler Terrible Towel. After conquering the lighthouse hike, we started heading back along the coastal route, and saw many of the suburbs where wealthy expats choose to live such as Camps Bay. Our day finished off with a stop in the Bo Kapp district of the city, where all of the houses are painted in the famous colorful exteriors, that you will often see in advertisements for Cape Town tourism. Simply an amazing day, filled with sights, history, and an unbelievable amount of culture. We still had 3 more days with which to enjoy this country.

Breaking a Cardinal Rule

The number 1 thing most people including Gillian, who are familiar with Cape Town told me I needed to do, was visit Table Mountain. My second day was the day I would make this happen, but my need to always go big, did not serve me well on this day. As much research as I try to do on a place I am visiting, you must always temper your decisions with caution. Table Mountain is a mountain right in the city, that allows you to take a cable car to the top, where you have an incredible 360-degree view of the entire city. It also allows those more adventurous, the ability to hike to the top of the mountain if that is more to your liking. I'll admit I was intrigued by the whole hiking concept, but wanted to make sure I knew what I was getting into. The South African Parks & Recreation website listed the hike as an "easy", meandering trail that would take about 1 ½ hours to the top. They recommended hiking up, and taking the cable car back down, to get the full experience. I would have thought hiking down would have been the easier option, but who was I to argue with the Parks & Rec Association. So, I headed out to the Mountain, bought my one-way cable car ticket, and proceeded to the trail head. Normally I would not do this by myself, but it was pretty popular, and was listed as easy, so I was in good shape.

I walked about a ½ mile when I arrived at the trail head, and looked at the map for the path to the top. The map even provided SOS information you could dial on your phone if you experienced any problems, "I got this". I started up the mountain, and about 15 minutes in discovered that my definition of easy & meandering was very different from what the Parks & Rec definition was. This was in my opinion a challenging ascent over rocks and very little established paths. Making things even more concerning was the lack of other hikers on the trail, bar the occasional person coming down that would pass me. I was in reality hiking alone, and that is the most egregious mistake a person can make. About half way into my ascent, I discovered that I had no cell phone service in that area, so if I needed any assistance, it would not have made a difference. I only noticed this because I was recording videos of the ascent, and those videos were capturing my fear, and my heightened sense of urgency to make it to the top. I had gone too far to quit, and surely, I was getting close to the top. The pinnacle of my concern was that the top of the mountain was still shrouded in mist, and wasn't even visible, so I could not really gauge how far I still had to go. A couple hiking down passed me by, and told me I was about 30 minutes from the top. Excited to hear, but physically exhausted, I pushed on, until I could tell I was nearing the top based on the temperature change, as it had gotten significantly colder. True to their word, the hikers were spot on, and about 30 minutes later, I arrived at the top, and my anxiety level dropped back down to a normal level. A small walk towards the cable car station, where the look-out points where, and I could see why everyone told me I had to visit Table Mountain. The views were spectacular, and my camera was in full use at this point.

I spent about 30 minutes total filming and taking pictures at the top, then decided it was time to descend, thankful that I had the ticket for the cable car to go back down. I knew I had not used good judgement choosing to hike to the top solo, but fortunately, everything turned out ok. Part of living the adventurous life I do, is the ability to learn from mistakes, and not ignore them should there be a next time. It took me 2 hours to hike to the top, and 6 minutes to ride back down. A huge time disparity to be sure, but a lifetime of memories that went with the experience. Hiking Table Mountain has become another mountain I have overcome in life, and that's what keeps me going!

Culture

I could not travel to South Africa, and not learn more about its history, culture and struggle for democracy. Seemed the best way for me to do that was to take a trip to Robben Island, and visit a very robust wine region. I took the ferry ride out to Robben Island, which for those who are not familiar is the United States equivalent to Alcatraz. An island prison, where many political prisoners were kept for many years, most notably the home of Nelson Mandela for a long time. It wasn't until 1994 that South Africa had true democracy with free elections, as the governing body prior to that was by a white minority. The prison visit, and the stories were a very surreal experience, and to see the conditions that many men lived under, because of the search for equality, still highlights the progress needed for man to make. Robben Island has now been closed and is a tourist attraction designed to educate visitors of the realities and hardships that inmates were subjected to. The tours are actually conducted by former inmates,
who are the best resources to speak to the realities of those who had endured it.

My final day in Cape Town was to be a relaxing day in the Wine Country area, and visiting 4 different vineyards for a variety of tastings. If ever there was day that was ear marked for no drama, it had to be this right? Enter Kenya Airways again, to screw up my trip, more than they already had! I was supposed to flight out of Cape Town to Nairobi late that night for an overnight flight. My flight back to the USA wasn't until late the following night, so I had a long layover in Nairobi. This wasn't a big deal, because I could wait the layover out in the Sky Club lounge at the airport. The lounge had sleeping and showering facilities, along with food and beverage, so it would not be that uncomfortable for me.

As I was heading out to the Wine Country, I got a message that Kenya Airways canceled my flight for later that night, and re-booked me on a flight that left 4 days later. This time I wasn't pleased, patient, or willing to accept their "tough shit" attitude, like I did the first time. I called the reservation center in Kenya, and told them to put me on another flight, even if it was another carrier, but I had to be in Nairobi for my flight out tomorrow night. After about 15 minutes, and me making it very clear I knew my rights as a passenger, they placed me on a flight through Johannesburg the next morning. It was still inconvenient, but it would allow me to catch my international flight home. This of course required that I book another night of hotel, and re-schedule my airport transfer, but they did get me on a 7am flight the next morning.

With that crisis averted, I was able to enjoy the rest of my day, and visit some incredible wineries over the course of the day. I visited some small family wineries, and some large more commercial operations. One of the wineries actually had a game reserve on their property, as zebras and wildebeest could be seen from the tasting room. Another location had goats on the premises, that they used to provide milk for the many cheeses they manufactured right on the grounds. It was a beautiful sun shiny day, and I even purchased a couple of bottles for the ride home. I love the art of wine making, and have learned a lot about wines over the years, so this trip to another country's wine region was the end of a perfect 4 days in South Africa.

Given all the craziness and changes I had to endure on this trip, I still had one more milestone to achieve, and that was to get home. This day would be the longest travel sequence of my career, as I was about to embark on a 48-hour transit back to America. The route would take me from Cape Town, to Johannesburg, to Nairobi, to Paris and finally Los Angeles. All told, the trip would be about 18,000 kilometers in travel over the course of 2 days. A lot of coffee, a few drinks, some brief periods of dozing on an airplane, and witnessing a guy walking around in his bare feet at the Sky Club in Paris, were the extent of that final journey home. It took a while to get home, and recover from the effects of time changes, but soon, the African Adventure was in the books, and a foot note to another Mid Life Adventure.

Final Thoughts

Appearances are often deceiving, and what is usually presented on the surface, only tells part of the story. I had many people comment to me that they felt this was my greatest adventure in their eyes. The truth is, I could probably say that about all of my adventures, at one time or another. So, you might find it a bit surprising when I tell you that this trip could very well be my greatest adventure, but I would also have to tell you from a logistical perspective, it was my worst adventure. Clearly the problems I experienced with Kenya Airways were a big part of that. Having a significant portion of my trip completely canceled, and changes to my schedule, along with having to pivot on a dime, made for a heightened level of stress, that you don't associate with a vacation. Not only did Kenya Airways disrupt my travel plans, but trying to obtain a refund for services I did not receive, proved to be a lengthy process as well. There is no doubt my experience with them has left an indelible memory with me, which I would have no problem sharing for those who might ask.

This trip was amazing with what I got to experience, but it also had many elements that detracted from my overall appreciation of it. I guess if I have barometer of how successful a trip is, it is the overarching question I often ask myself "Would I ever go back". The answer here is yes & no! Would I ever go back to Kenya? While I never say never, my answer right now would be "probably not" There are always unforeseen circumstances that could bring me back, but if it was strictly my choice, I don't think I would. Let me say that I had a wonderful time, the safari was an incredible experience, the people that I met were great, but there were other things that I did not find great. The infrastructure outside of Nairobi, I found to be very lacking. Kenya is one of the wealthier countries in Africa, and yet, there is a huge underclass, and roads, buildings and other components of a developing country, seemed to be missing.

Would I return to South Africa? Without question the answer to that is yes! I found Cape Town to be an amazing experience, and one where I would love to see the rest of this diverse country. There will always be a point to where a traveler likens his experience to that which is more familiar on an everyday basis. Part of the joy of traveling is to experience different cultures, but we often confuse the notion of culture and poverty as one and the same. South Africa, like all other countries will have its moments, but I know that the potential for growth and improvement will always be there.

One additional question I need to ask myself is "Will I have the opportunity to see Victoria Falls again", in its pure form. I could easily make the decision to head back as a goal, but I'm not sure seeing that last natural wonder is that important to me, or if it was just having that accolade of saying I have seen all 7 wonders, that was really the driving force. Perhaps I did learn more about myself on this trip, than I originally thought?

Sunset on the Mara
Masai Mara, Kenya. May, 2021

Pride of Lions
Masai Mara, Kenya. May, 2021

Viewing a herd of elephants
Amboseli National Park, Kenya. May, 2021

Sunrise at the Harbor
Cape Town SA. June, 2021

The Summit of Table Mountain
Cape Town, SA.
June, 2021

12.

That's Amore

If there was one thing in my life that had currently fallen under the status of unfulfilled, it would be that I had not had the opportunity to share with my daughters, the experience of international travel. As they were growing up, we did some family vacations, including a cruise to Mexico, but nothing that I would classify as a true international adventure. They knew of my many adventures around the world, either for business, or things I may have done before they were born, and most recently, my travels during their post teenage years. Still, this was something that had been gnawing at me for a while. I would often ask them if they wanted to do a trip with me, however, some of the adventures I chose to do, never really appealed to their desires. I confess, that hiking mountains and volcanos, or exploring ancient ruins isn't big on most people's list, but it's what I do. I never wanted to give up hope on taking them on an adventure with me, and on Father's Day of 2021, we agreed to make it a reality before the end of the year.

During dinner, my daughter's Katie & Megan expressed a real desire to do something with me, but it had to be something they would enjoy as well. So, we kicked around some ideas, and places they wanted to see. I had mentioned that one place I wanted to go, but had never been to was Greece. Their eyes lit up like a full moon, with both of them saying, that is a place they would like to see. That became our starting point for what would eventually become known as the ***"Greco-Roman Adventure"***. An adventure that would go through many iterations and changes, along with some major family news, as we made a commitment to make this trip happen.

The reason that only two of my daughters were going on an adventure with me, is because before I left for Africa in the Spring, my oldest daughter Alissa, announced that she was going to have a baby, and my family would soon be blessed with our first grandchild. This was a joyous announcement, and one that would perhaps alter my own priorities in the coming months and years ahead. For obvious reasons, she would not

97

be able to join us on this trip, and while starting a family shifts your focus for the long term, I still have a goal that one day I can share a trip of this magnitude with her.

Now that we had a destination in mind, the actual planning needed to start. We decided to travel over the Thanksgiving holiday, which provided a few months of getting ready, and financially planning for the trip. Not surprising, I took the lead on finding the best air fares, things to do, and mapping out an itinerary. I knew that I wanted to spend a couple of days in Athens, but also wanted to spend a few days on a Greek Island. The girls were ok with this, but then it was time to compromise. Having never been to Greece before, I wanted to expand the trip and visit Northern Greece in the area of Thessaly. This was of little interest to the girls, and I could tell, that this part of the trip was not that exciting for them. At that point my wheels starting turning, and my knowledge of geography kicked in, which would be the final piece of this trifecta trip.

Wanting to squeeze as much variety into this trip as I could, I looked at a couple of ideas to see if we could make them work. What jumped out on the page at me was Rome, Italy. With just a 90-minute flight from Athens, we could add an entirely different culture, cuisine, and history in a few short days. The girls agreed, and the itinerary was set. We would have 10 days in Greece & Italy, and one added surprise, that I would share with them, once I confirmed the plane tickets. I had been to Italy many years earlier, and truthfully wasn't overly impressed. I'll admit I was in my 20's back then, and culture and history took a back seat to running around and partying in Europe. I knew however, this was important to my girls, and that was taking precedent on this trip.

As I have done on many of my recent adventures, I looked for an opportunity to travel on a foreign air carrier, in hopes of possibly including a brief stopover in another city, on the way to our destination. This time, the optimal choice would be Air France, as they had a schedule that would give us a 9-hour layover in Paris on the way to Athens. That was enough time to catch a train into the city, look around at a few of the famous sights, and experience just a little bit more of Europe. I had flown Air France on my return from Kenya, and was very impressed with their service, and I knew the girls would love seeing Paris, even if only for a few hours. We finalized the dates, booked the tickets for a good price, (that got even better as time went on) and were confirmed for our trip. This trip was going to happen, and each of us was brimming with excitement.

Minus One

With all the excitement that my daughters and I had going into this new adventure, we managed to get a bit sidetracked regarding the elements of the pandemic. Travel had been growing, and there was much less talk and thankfully less fear about traveling. Still, countries were playing it very safe, and many were using the ability to travel as an incentive to persuade people to get vaccinated. This wasn't an issue for me because, as I had mentioned previously, I decided to get the vaccine for my trip to Africa earlier in the year. However, neither of my daughters had gotten it up to this point. We were looking at two countries to visit, being Greece and Italy, and in addition, we had planned a long layover in Paris on the way over. With our plan being to leave the Paris airport, and venture into the city, we had to take into consideration the entry requirements for the country of France.

Nothing about Covid has been normal or consistent, and the entry requirements for each country was the proof of that. Each had a slightly different requirement, some required a vaccine, some did not, some required a test, some did not. In the end, it all became very confusing. No matter what the requirements, both of my girls had a big decision to make. Both of them were adamant about not wanting to get the vaccine, but were willing to adhere to the testing requirements for entry into each country. The situation changed when France amended the requirement for entry to only vaccinated travelers, and the real possibility of the other countries doing the same, seemed increasingly likely. Now it became a situation where you either get the vaccine, or you cannot go. There are many things I have been able to figure out when traveling, and ways to work the system, however, there was nothing I could do to circumvent the criteria a country places on entry. Faced with this decision, Katie decided she would forgo the trip, while Megan decided to go ahead and get the vaccine. I offered my opinion about this trip and any future trips that might come along the way, and I felt that the vaccine would only become more of a requirement. As much as I wanted Katie to join us, I respected her stance, and am proud that she did what she felt was best for her. I know she thought about the pros and cons, and while I may not have come to the same conclusion, the decision she came to was made by her, and not someone else. I only hope that she and I will have an opportunity in the future to have a great adventure.

The Adventure Begins

About 6 weeks before Megan and I would depart for Europe, my beautiful little granddaughter **"Tatum"** came into the world. This was indeed a new adventure for me, as she was my 1st grandchild. I have always struggled with the concept of being a grandfather. Not that I didn't want to, but more because I often still view myself through very young eyes. I have many friends who became so fixated on being a grandparent, to the point of almost being obsessed by it. Maybe I was a bit afraid that I might not be a good grandparent? Whatever I may have been feeling, it all became mute when Tatum arrived. This tiny little life breathed a whole new adventure into me, and while I believe I will still view my life as one big adventure, it is now complimented by one tiny adventure. There is no doubt that some things will change in me, but there will be many new things that I will undertake with this young lady. My travel adventures come and go, but this is one adventure I plan to experience for quite a long time.

Soon Megan and I were headed to LAX for our flight to France. I wanted this trip to be so special for her, and I was going to pull out all the stops to make it happen. I got us into the Air France lounge at LAX, where we were able to grab a nice meal and some pre-flight drinks. We had a nice champagne toast to start the Greco-Roman Adventure, and I was hoping it would help relaxer her for the upcoming long flight. A 10-hour flight is the longest single flight she had ever been on, and if you are tense, time tends to drag on and on. The flight over was without incident, and soon we landed in Paris. After a relatively easy process through immigration, we grabbed the train at the airport, and sped into the heart of the city. We had about 9 hours to see as much as we could, and we didn't waste a minute of it. We got off the train at the station right outside of Notre Dame cathedral. Still mostly covered in scaffolding from the fire 2 years ago, it was nonetheless a spectacular sight. We grabbed a few pictures, then started walking the streets of Paris towards our ultimate destination, the Eiffel Tower.

As we walked along the Seine River, we stopped at the Louvre Museum. Megan really wanted to see the Mona Lisa painting, however, with full Covid restrictions in place, you had to reserve a time for entrance, and you had to produce a freshly taken Covid test available only at local pharmacies around the city. With all the requirements, we would never have had enough time to visit the museum inside. A few photos of the Louvre, and we were on our way through the Place de la Concorde. From there we could see the Arc de Triomphe on the Champs Elysées. It was a beautiful sunshine day in Paris, if only a little on the cold side, but I could see Megan's expressions, and just how impressed she was with the Parisian culture.

As we headed over to the left bank of the river, we could see the Eiffel Tower in the distance, and picked up our pace to make good time. It had been about 17 years in between visits to Paris for me, and I was curious to see how much the city had changed in that time, if at all. We arrived at the tower, and I could immediately see what Covid had brought to town. Much of the park that the tower sits on, used to be open where you could walk right under the tower itself, and see the many steps one could climb to the 2nd level view point. Much of that was now closed, and the park was reduced to mostly foot paths, as you could no longer sit on the grass. I found that very much had changed since my last visit in 2002, and I would be so bold as to say, not for the better.

Still, it was the Eiffel Tower, and my daughter was getting a tourist lesson, even if it was an accelerated one at that. We had reached the late afternoon, and we wanted a little time for a snack and some souvenir hunting, so we started to head back towards the Metro train after we grabbed something to eat. Meg had designs on a French Beret, but couldn't find one that appealed to her. We got back on the Metro and headed back to Charles De Gaulle airport for our flight down to Athens later that night. We finished our day with a visit to the Air France lounge before the flight, and topped off a very busy day in the city of light with what else, French champagne. Soon we were off to Athens to learn about the cradle of Western civilization.

Plato's iPhone

Megan and I arrived in Athens very late at night, or early in the morning if you prefer, so the immigration and customs process went pretty smoothly. Fortunately, our airport transfer was waiting there for us, and soon we were whisked away heading to our hotel at 2am. One of the big challenges when traveling to a place you have never been before, is choosing the right place to stay. As much research as you can possibly do, you are never quite sure if where you are staying, will be convenient for your goals. Using public transportation, or walking a little bit of a distance is always something I enjoy doing, but this trip wasn't just about me, so I had to take Megan's considerations into account as well. When I look for a place to stay, I look for accessibility to mass transportation, or are the things I want to see within walking distance. Turns out the hotel I chose for Athens, was actually both. With a little research, I came across a property called PI Athens. This was a very small property, it only had 8 rooms, but those rooms had an unobstructed view of the Acropolis. When Meg and I arrived around 3:00am, we were able to check in, and go right to the room. I pulled back the curtain from the window, and could not believe my eyes. Out in the distance, lit up in bright lights, I could see the Parthenon, at the top of the Acropolis. The pictures on the Internet did not lie, and were exactly as portrayed. We needed to get some rest, because day 1 in Athens would be a busy one.

We gave ourselves a few extra hours in the morning to sleep, but needed to be ready to go by 10am. I have found the best way to get my bearings in a new place, is to take a local walking tour. I booked a Free Tour through a company I have had success with during past adventures. I had a great experience in Cairo, and other places using this service, so I thought this would be a good way to acclimate. We were supposed to meet the walking tour at 10:00am, but because we got a bit lost, and had to walk a little further than anticipated, we arrived 5 minutes late. Normally this is no big deal, however, we were unable to locate the guide, and never got to participate in the tour. Because of that, I became the emergency tour guide, and took the lead on showing my daughter a city that was new to both of us. The plan was to experience the city a little bit, and make our way to the Acropolis. After all, this is the big draw when you come to Athens. We grabbed a couple of those "hope on, hop off" bus tickets, that would allow us to take out time, but still make our way to the Acropolis.

After a few stops, the next stop was the Acropolis, and a checklist item was about to be achieved, along with a huge trip changing set back. After taking a small hike to see the Acropolis from a distance, we headed up the path that would take us right to the main structures, the Parthenon and The Temple of Athena among others. This is where the perfect storm occurred, and changed the trajectory of this trip. The Acropolis is an outdoor venue, but, showing a current Covid vaccine certificate was required to enter, as was wearing a mask. As we arrived, it started to rain, so I had to set down my backpack, get out a mask, and my certificate to walk through the gate. During this time, I set down my phone subconsciously, and never picked it up, while needing to pull out an umbrella. I'll admit, I was beyond frustrated because of the vaccine & mask requirements to enter an outdoor museum, especially since the mask could be removed, once you went through the turnstile. My emotions got the best of me, and I totally lost track of my thoughts that I had set my phone down. Needless to say, when I recognized it was missing a few minutes later, I knew it was gone for good. Even retracing my steps proved fruitless, and checking the front gate for a lost & found process, was an absolute joke.

During the trip so far, I had been focusing on protecting my camera, and accessories, because you always hear about guarding your expensive items when traveling. I think we all take our phones for granted these days, and in actuality, my phone cost more than the camera I was so focused on protecting. I suppose you could say, hey, it's just a phone, until you realize how much we rely on our phones. Our entire itinerary for this trip was on my phone, not to mention all of my banking and credit card APP's, thus my immediate fear was that access could be gained to my personal accounts. Tickets, confirmations for tours, emails etc., were all lost, or at least not in the palm of my hand. Because of this, my stress level heightened, and I was pretty much consumed for the remainder of the day.

We now had to rely on Megan's phone for a lot of the things that needed to get done. If ever I truly felt like I was back in the early days of civilization, it was now. In the birthplace of Western philosophy, I was concerned about my digital life. Still, we needed to explore the Acropolis, and in particular, the Parthenon close up. The fact that I was standing among structures that were over 2000 years old, and seeing how well preserved, and advanced for their time they were, was mind numbing. I took a step back and watched Megan absorb all of this culture. Most young folks these days, don't seem to have an appreciation for history, and its significance into the development of society, but Megan is one who does. When it comes to studying history, and culture, she is the most like me in that regard.

After exploring the Acropolis grounds, we headed back to our hotel, where I was able to get on my iPad, change my passwords for banking and credit information, and remotely have my lost phone wiped of any data. There is no doubt that I really became aware just how much of my life is dependent upon a hand-held device. We can debate whether that is a good thing, or bad thing, but what wasn't debatable was that I would be without a phone for the next 9 days. If that wasn't bad enough, I already had in my mind, this was first thing I had to address when I returned home, and my vacation had just started. The 1st 24 hours after losing my phone put me in a bad frame of mind, and I felt bad, because Megan endured some of that, but once I knew my personal & financial interests were safe, I started to make the best of it.

Our 2nd day was more at leisure, as we both wanted to see the city of Athens on our own timetable, as well as take in a little culinary culture, and some shopping. Since we didn't have a schedule, we were able to take our time and absorb as much or as little as we wanted. We spent time checking out the academic elements of the city, with the Museums, and the University of Athens, complete with the statues of Plato & Socrates out front. The architecture in Athens, like most of Europe, is very grand with columns, and temple style designs. I of course had my brochures that described what we were looking at, and Megan focused on proper lighting for the best camera angles. We took a lunch break and tried a few Greek favorites including Gyros and stuffed grape leaves. Rather surprising was that many restaurants in Athens were requiring proof of vaccination to eat outdoors! I was expecting some of the restaurants to enforce this requirement for indoor dining, but requiring it for outdoor dining was definitely unexpected. A little shopping later on allowed me to grab a few new souvenirs for my collection of memorabilia back home, and a few gag gift ideas for friends as well.

What I had been told prior to my arrival in Athens is that it is a neat city, but 2 days is plenty of time to see and do the essentials, and that was pretty spot on. One thing I still wanted to do was some night photography and video of the Acropolis. Megan opted to take a late afternoon nap, and I headed over to the Acropolis after dark. As I started to get my bearings of the city, I decided to walk over, and it took me about 20 minutes, which wasn't bad at all. The weather was fine, albeit a bit cool, but no rain. The sight of the entire Acropolis lit up with the flood lights was very impressive, and I made sure to take plenty of pictures from a variety of angles and viewpoints. I had checked another item off of my personal list of things I would like to see in the world, and this was certainly one of them. It wasn't a late night by design, as we had a very early departure the next morning, that would start phase two of this 3 phase adventure. It was time for us to travel to one of the most popular of all the Greek Isles.

Welcome To Atlantis

As the 5:00am hour arrived, it was time for us to depart our hotel in Athens to Piraeus Port, where Meg and I would board a ferry to take us to the Island of Santorini. Santorini is probably the most famous of the Greek Isles, although Mykonos and Rhodes may disagree with that sentiment. Most people who have either been to, or have a desire to see, often mention Santorini as the spot they have on their must-see list. It is by far the island that is included on most cruise ship itineraries as well. We were set for a 3 night stay on the island, and although this day was Thanksgiving Day in America, I was happy to trade turkey for lamb on this day. Soon we were sailing on the Aegean Sea, on a day that turned out to be perfect for sailing, as one of the few times the sun was actually out for the entire day. I booked us 2 business class tickets on the ferry, which gave us access to a quieter area of the ship, with very comfortable seating, and many amenities. Though the ship itself was sparsely populated, we had about 7 hours of sailing, so I wanted us to be comfortable for that time.

We arrived around 3:00pm, and reserved a ride up the side of the mountain to our hotel, which was located in the capital of the island, in the town called Thira. As I usually do, I started studying my literature, and learned that the island of Santorini is believed to be the actual location of the mythical city of Atlantis. There is a wide held believe that volcanic eruptions thousands of years ago, created the island, which in turn destroyed the Lost Continent of Atlantis. Truth or not, it made for a fun piece of trivia to start this part of the trip off with.

Traveling to a Greek Isle at the end of November gave me no illusions that this would be a beach, water and summer style vacation, but I was caught off guard by the effect of the seasonal limitations we would soon discover. During the Winter season, only about 25% of the island's business, hotels, restaurants etc., would remain open. It was as if a small number of services were made available, to serve those who lived on the island year-round. This lack of open business made for some positives, as well as negatives. One of the constant draw backs I had always heard about Santorini was the crowds that flocked to the tourist places such as Sunset in the town of Oui. The Caldera (cliff) is a walking path along a great stretch of the cliff along the island that many people can walk from town to town. This walkway is very narrow, and is for the most part made of cobblestone. In high tourist season, these walkways get incredibly crowded. That was not going to be the case, as there were relatively few tourists that we saw for our entire stay. On the negative side, my vision of being on a Greek Isle, and hearing a plethora of restaurants all playing live Greek music was not to be. Most of the night time entertainment places were closed for the season, and would not open back up for about 4 months.

With practically the whole island to ourselves (figuratively), Meg and I had a full day of sightseeing around the island planned. Yes, it was just us on this tour, which although not planned, became a private tour. Trying to fit as much as possible into this day, we would experience a stop at a local winery, a visit to the Black Sand Beach, a small hike to the lighthouse, a stop at the famed blue domed church, and a finale in the town of Oui, to watch the sunset over the Aegean. The weather cooperated until it didn't, as we endured sunshine mixed with light rain, and a nonstop 50 mph wind, that made my video and picture taking problematic. We each managed to pick up a couple bottles of local Greek wine to bring home, got some amazing pictures of the black sand and cliff formations along the sea, and arrived just in time for the sunset at Oui, (pronounced EE AH). All of the pictures, and tourist advertisements for Santorini, never leave out the blue domed churches, as there are dozens of them all over the island. Suddenly, I realized I was now among them, and not just viewing from the Internet, but actually standing among them, and capturing memories with my camera & video equipment.

We knew we were getting close to sunset while we walked along the Caldera, as you could see other people gathering at the view point, all waiting to take that sunset picture that this island has become famous for. Slowly the sun dropped to just below the horizon, and my camera shutter started firing off, along with every other would be photographer. I was able to get some video footage as well, but the strong wind made it almost impossible to hold the camera steady, and the audio sounded like a true hurricane. Both Megan and I posed for photos with the sunset as the backdrop, and a lasting memory, if not a predictable tourist event to end our day.

One of the new realities of traveling during, and post pandemic, is undoubtedly the hassle of coordinating Covid testing into the agenda. This is a very real part of traveling, at least for the foreseeable future. Handling this requires planning, just as much as any sightseeing tour or activity on any international journey. Because we would be flying from Santorini to Rome Italy in the morning, we needed to take a Covid test the day before. Fortunately, our final day in Santorini was low key, and I will credit the Greek Government for making the testing process extremely easy, and inexpensive. Local pharmacies have a small table setup, you fill out the form, pay your 10 Euros, and let them swab your nose. We got our results back in about 30 minutes, and to no surprise, we were both negative. After a little shopping we were walking back to the hotel along the Caldera, and happened to catch the ordaining service of a new Greek Orthodox Bishop, at one of the main churches. I love to watch other cultures embrace their history, and honor the traditions, much more than finding ways to be offended by something, like we tend to be in America. We reached the end of our stay in Santorini, and with one shot of Ouzo, prepared ourselves to start phase 3 of the trip, the Roman part of this adventure.

You say "Carbonairo" I say "Carbonaro"

It was to be a relatively easy flight from Santorini to Rome via Athens, but nothing during Covid times should be taken for granted. Negative tests aside, a whole bunch of digital certificates and online forms need to be filled out these days, and each country has their own set they require. So, when Aegean airlines told me I didn't have the correct form uploaded, it created a mini tailspin. No problem right, "just download the form to your phone", and you are good to go. Except for the fact that I had no phone, thanks to my miscue in Athens. Megan would have to download the form for herself, then I had to use her phone to download a form for myself. This was 20 extra stressful minutes that reminded me, how much my life depends on a palm held device! 2 uploads and 1 deep breath later, we were on the plane. Much to Megan's chagrin, Santorini to Athens was a small propeller plane, and while that was not a real issue for me, this would be her 1st time on a small plane. The rest of the flight to Rome was uneventful, and soon we were clearing immigration and customers in the Country of Italy. This time on arrival, the car service ordered in advance was nowhere present. Under normal circumstances, I would pull out my phone, look up the itinerary, and call the service to find out where the driver was. These however were not normal circumstances, and once again, the lack of a mobile communication device proved troublesome. At this point, the stress of not having my go to device, along with just the miscue of the driver not being at the meeting space, was becoming more stressful than I am comfortable with. My temper was short with Megan, and I felt frustrated with all these little nuances. Was all this travel during the pandemic, and all the cancelations, and inconveniences laid at the feet of Covid, catching up with me? It was a fair question to ask of myself, and even for someone else to ask of me.

We started to walk down past a few other baggage claim entrances, and something caused me to look left, and there I saw a gentleman holding a small sign that said "Paul Foster", it was our driver. He showed up at the wrong door, and after about 15 minutes of uncertainty, we were on our way into the city to our hotel. I had booked a hotel that was near the Fontana de Trevi (Trevi Fountain). I choose it because of its central and walkable location to much of the key spots in Rome. After we checked in, we had much of the afternoon to explore on foot the Eternal City.

We walked past the Trevi Fountain, then made our way towards the Roman Forum, and ultimately ended up in front of the Colosseum, which inevitably led to a series of photographic poses, and angles. My little girl was experiencing the culture, history, and soon the cuisine of Italy.

It had been 31 years since I was last in Rome, and being completely honest, much of that trip was a blur. There was something different about this time for me, as I started to take a more philosophical look at the city, rather than looking for the nearest bar, like 30 years ago. We were looking to grab a late lunch, but could not decide where or what to eat. The fact is, most every place had a variety of pasta dishes, and a multitude of different style pizzas. I knew from our lunch break, that we would not go hungry in Rome.

Food has always been the great unknown for me, and my ability to dive right into local cuisine, is often guarded at best. This timidness rolls all the way back to 1989, where on a trip to Rio de Janeiro, I became ill with food poisoning. I have NEVER been the same since that time, and always remain very cautious when trying new foods. I know that this detracts from the adventure, but the lingering memories of that illness, still reverberate with me as if it were yesterday. All of my trips around the world have presented me with great culinary experiences, and some not so great. I loved the food in China, but not so much in Tibet. I was surprised at how well I gravitated towards the foods of Nepal and Egypt, but was very unimpressed with Russian and Kenyan food. My approach always ends up taking a wait and see attitude, but in Italy, I felt like I could dive in, and feel pretty safe about it.

For our 1st evening in Rome, I really went to my bag of adventure tricks and found what would turn out to be one of the most enjoyable local tours I have ever booked. I found a small tour company that offered a nighttime electric bicycle tour through Rome, and knew this was a Mid Life Adventure. The tour started at 7:00pm, and at 6:00pm, Megan was sound asleep well into an afternoon nap. I had to wake her, and ultimately drag her kicking and screaming, as her preference was to just blow this tour off, and sleep. I was having none of that, and after dealing with her scowls, and comments, we arrived at the meeting point. A few minutes of instructions, a couple of safety helmets, a last-minute couple add on to the tour, and we were on our way. The problem was that the rain was on its way too, but that would not dampen this evening. This was a 4-hour tour, that literally visited every Roman landmark & Piazza you could think of. This was not just a bicycle ride through a big city, but a ride through the small streets and alleys not visited by many tourist seeking individuals. I remember turning left then right down these little side streets, sometimes having to stop and let someone cross the street, then make another right turn only to come face to face with St. Peters Square in Vatican City. No traffic, no horn honking or traffic signals on this trip, just a leisurely bike ride through the small streets of a well-lit city.

Half way through the trip, the tour stopped at a local café where they presented us with a variety of local meats, cheeses and wine for tasting. This was included in the tour, and as we sat and talked with other members of the tour from different countries, I remember thinking to myself, this was exactly the type of experience that I wanted to someday share with my daughters. At the end of the tour Megan had said to me walking back to the hotel that she was so glad we did the bike experience, and that's when I knew my dream of sharing this with my daughter, had become a reality, on a late November rainy night in the city of Rome.

An Ordinary Miracle

Throughout the planning of this adventure, I really focused on doing things that the girls wanted to do. I made suggestions from an experience standpoint, but they had their own agendas as well. Having to compromise on an adventure agenda was a new experience for me, and something I was really out of practice with. I had become so used to traveling solo, that the running joke was, if I didn't have a good time, there was only one person to blame. With that in mind, there were some items on this trip that if I were traveling solo, I would have by passed on. Mainly because I had already done most of them on a previous trip. There was however one thing that I identified from the very beginning. If I was going to visit Rome again, I wanted to make a side trip to see the ruins of Pompeii, and climb Mt. Vesuvius. Located outside the city of Naples, which was just an hour by train from Rome, Pompeii was the city covered in lava when Mt. Vesuvius erupted in the year 79AD. The city was completely covered, and many people were buried alive. Over the last few hundred years, the city was discovered, and excavation and preservation of the city had started.

I found a tour that allowed Megan and I to see the excavated ruins, and then hike to the top of Mt. Vesuvius, and see inside the crater. Much like my trip to Volcan Paricutin in Mexico, a year earlier, my fascination with climbing mountains & volcanos would be realized again. This was something that Megan probably could have left off her itinerary, however once I explained the historical significance of Pompeii, her love of history kicked in, and she was much more on board with doing this side excursion. A couple of in expensive train tickets from Rome, and 70 minutes later we were on our way. Sadly, it was time for another itinerary pivot, much to my chagrin. Throughout the entire trip, the weather had been on again, off again, and today was very much off! It was raining very hard when we got to Naples, as such the climbing of Mt. Vesuvius portion, was canceled. I was not going to get to climb history's most famous volcano. This was hard, because up till now, all the delays and changes I had experienced on my trips over the last couple of years, we more covid related. This was a weather problem, and there was nothing I could do to control this. Because we were on a tight schedule, I could not postpone to another day when the weather might have been more favorable. The reality of this was, I chose a bad time to travel to this area of Europe, from a weather standpoint. I usually research the weather patterns, and the best times to go, when I select an adventure. I think I got caught up in cheap air fares, and just didn't research the weather factor for this trip. Even with all the places I have traveled to, it was a reminder that I don't know everything.

We had to take a local commuter rail from the Naples city station out to Pompeii, which took about 35 minutes. Once we got our tickets to enter the site, the rain started again. It was clear this would be a stop and start situation all day long. We walked the streets of Pompeii, and saw many neighborhood homes, and places that appeared to be local businesses of the time. I could see that Megan was very interested in all of the history, and the stories behind everyday life in 79AD. We came across a section where they had plaster casts of actual bodies that were found preserved during the excavation. We also saw an extensive amount of pottery work & tools that were fashioned during that time. Some surprising things we discovered was that indoor plumbing was available, albeit in a crude form, but nonetheless, something that was used almost 2000 years ago. We were able to visit the House of Octavius, who later would become the very first Roman Emperor. After several hours of walking around in the rain, I started to lose patience, and had more than my fill of ruins. I was being unfair to Megan, as she was enjoying all of this, while I was trying to protect expensive camera equipment from the rain. I gutted it out, and soon she told me, she had seen all things she wanted to. I know she really took a lot away from this experience, and learned that back in those 24 hours of 79AD, it was an ordinary miracle, as it is often referred to as.

Since we had some extra time, we decided to head back into Naples and try some pizza, as Naples is listed as the birth place of pizza. We found a little café, and each of us tried a different individual pizza, along with some wine. The pizza itself I thought was ok, but this was more about experiencing it, in the city believed to be the its home. After a leisurely dinner, it was time to head back to the train station for the ride back to Rome. It had been a long, but productive & educational day, as most of the days on this trip were. Both of us would sleep well tonight, and we would need it as we were coming up on our last sightseeing day of our trip, with, you guessed it, one added surprise.

Our final sightseeing day would include a slower pace for shopping, a trip to the Vatican Museum, some cuisine, a special guest, and the now obligatory Covid test, so we could return home. We got an early start, and set out for some souvenirs and some Italian wines. Very close to the hotel we came across a couple of places to get those all-important trinkets for family members at home. We happened on a small wine and specialty foods store, and decided to check it out. The shop name was Enotrevi Sri, and the owner was a wonderful lady, who was very helpful to us. We would soon find out just how helpful a little later in the day. Megan and I bought some wine, and she bought some authentic Italian spices, and butters. This was the kind of shop you could spend an entire day in, and the fact that it is family run, made it that much more special.

One of the many blessings I have had over the years, is the numerous friends I have made around the world whenever I travel. I still communicate with many of them on a regular basis, through various social media apps. I would someday like to be able to arrange a reunion with all the people I have met, in a neutral setting. For now, the best I could do was to arrange to meet up with my friend Viktur Andrusik. I met Viktur back in 2017, while we were on a trip to China & Tibet. He lives in Hungary, and while I thought it might be a long shot, I asked him if he would like to come down to Rome to spend a day with Megan and me. One of the most enticing elements of Europe is that countries are so close together, that you can often visit several in a single day. I kept in touch as to our progress and a few days before, he confirmed he could come down to Rome, and meet up with us. I didn't say anything initially to Megan, because I wasn't sure if he could make it, but when he confirmed, I told her. I wanted to share with her, the experience of having global friends from around the world. Someone whom I had met 4 years ago in Asia, was coming to Italy to spend the day with us. Though Viktur is much younger than I am, he shares my passion for international travel, and I hope that fire never dies within him. He appears in the picture on the back cover of my last book, and played a very big part on this adventure.

We met Viktur in front of the Trevi fountain, and started heading toward Vatican City. It was rather apropos that on our last day of the trip, the sun would be shining, and temperature was mild for early December. Our destination was the Vatican Museum, and after much confusion about where we would buy our tickets, and falling for a tourist scam, thinking we had bought discount tickets, we finally found our way inside the museum. Like most famous museums around the world, the Vatican has tons of displays that appear to be relevant, and usually one big calling card. In the case of the Vatican Museum, it is Michelangelo's Sistine Chapel. Also, like most other museums, they make you go through the whole thing, until you get to the famous display. We had to walk through the entire museum in a one-way path. Meg took her time, and I let her have a run with my camera, as she wanted to take pictures from a variety of different angles. Finally, we made it into the chapel, and of course you are not allowed to take pictures of the famous ceiling. With the chapel as crowded as it was, I started taking photos in an incognito manner. Since I was firing off the shutter without actually lining up the shots, I had to rely on my equipment taking those pictures blindly. How lucky I was that some of the impromptu pictures captured probably the most famous fresco "The Creation of Adam". All in all, we probably spent about 2 hours in the museum and St. Peters Square, but we still had more to do.

It was well into the afternoon hours, and we all had a desire for some
food. I think one of the biggest challenges in Italy, was where to choose
to eat. Tons of cafes lined the streets, and they all serve a variation of the
same thing, pasta. On a previous trip to Rome, Viktur had remembered
a place that he liked very much, so we headed in that direction. Along
the way we came across the Spanish Steps, and just had to take some
pictures. The place we were looking for was not open, so we found
another café, and tried a little bit of everything. The whole trip I was
amazed at Megan's knowledge of Italian cooking, particularly the sauces.
I wasn't sure if she had boned up on this information prior to the trip, or
has a hidden passion, but her knowledge proved very helpful. We took
our time with dinner, and enjoyed everything, but we had a 6:00pm
appoint for that Covid test, so we started off for the clinic.

Taking these negative tests has become a real hinderance, but it is also
a reality now. I don't foresee those requirements going away anytime
soon. Up till now, the testing has gone pretty smoothly, but every
country has their own process and requirements. Even though we had an
appointment, we still ended up waiting about 30 minutes. The process of
testing was pretty easy, and we would have the results in about an hour.
No sweat right! We could not finish off this trip without one more wrench
tossed in for good measure. We walked back to the hotel, and said our
goodbye's to Viktur, who was staying for a few additional days. We had to
now try to fit everything into suitcases, after a full day of shopping.

I checked my email and saw that the Covid test result had come back.
The form was sent in Italian and neither of us could read it, so we didn't
know the result, or what to do with it. The front desk of the hotel was of
absolutely no help, or possibly he just didn't want to be bothered. We
had to upload this form to the Italian Health Ministry, a web site also in
Italian, with no English option. As per my usual, I started to get stressed,
then took a deep breath, and came up with an idea. Back to the quaint
little wine shop Enotrevi Sri, where the owner was more than happy
to translate the form for us, and help us upload the form. We were so
grateful for her assistance, that Megan decided to spend some more
money, for a few more authentic Italian foods. Per my usual routine, on

a final night, I like to do a bit of street photography. That brought us to a Gelato house, where I had the true Italian experience with my daughter. Our 11-day adventure was coming to an end, and I realized that one of the things I have wanted to give my daughter was complete, and another life's goal reached.

Final Thoughts

I've tried to put into words what this experience was like for me, and for my daughter, but some things are hard to sum up in words, but are best defined by emotions and feelings. I can only hope that Megan took away a huge amount of knowledge, and passion for other cultures. We had just stormed through 3 countries, and saw things that I wasn't sure I would be able to show her. Sharing a glass of wine, a gelato cone, a Gyro, and standing before architecture dating back thousands of years, was everything I thought it would be with her.

I also learned some things about myself on this trip too. Having experienced a functional setback right at the beginning of the trip (Cell Phone), I need to learn how to handle these situations, and pivot better than I did. Stressing when these things happened isn't going to resolve the situation any faster. My Type "A" personality was on full display this trip, and I think it did detract a little bit with Megan. The other thing I need to reconcile is do I want to continue to travel alone, or with someone else. I have long said that it would be nice to find someone who shares my passions for these adventurous endeavors, but when I did have someone, I felt constrained. Have I gotten so used to calling all the shots on my activities, that I lost sight that this trip was hers as well? We did butt heads on a couple of instances, and not all the things were her fault. I was just as much at fault for some of those things. There were several things that I wanted to do, that she had little or no interest in doing, and that resulted in disagreements. Could it be that maybe my youngest daughter is more like me than I ever realized? Her passion for travel, history, food, and even photography rivals that of my own. Challenges aside, I would welcome the opportunity to have another adventure with her, or any of my daughters, and that my friends is **Amore**.

Megan & I having a quick bite in front of the Eiffel Tower
Paris, FR. November, 2021

The splendor of the Parthenon at night
Athens GR. November, 2021

The blue domed churches of Santorini
Santorini, GR. November 2021

The Caldera of Oui
Santorini, GR.
November, 2021

Fontana de Trevi (Trevi Fountain)
Rome, IT. December, 2021

The Colosseum
Rome, IT. December, 2021

Vatican City at Night
Rome, IT. December, 2021

Mt. Vesuvius in Winter
Pompeii, IT. December 2021

Dinner with my friend Viktur
Rome, IT. December, 2021

Megan & I enjoying a Gelato
Rome, IT. December, 2021

13.

Jesus Take the Wheel

Everyone at one time or another has probably been in a situation where they feel stagnant in their life, and look to seek some changes. It is not uncommon for the feelings to become even more prominent at the end of a calendar year. Given the human toll the previous 2 years had taken on everybody, most people might just long for a return to normal. For me, it became something more than just the traditional set of New Year's Resolutions. I had been very active during the pandemic with travel and other adventures, but still something seemed to be missing.

Before I left for the Greco-Roman adventure, a position at my company had opened up that caught my interest. It was a leadership position in an area that I had worked in years before, but had been away from since I had been with my current company. I really enjoyed my job and what I had accomplished the last 3 years helping customers improve their travel programs. Finding a job that you can be passionate about is something that is not always easy to secure, and I wondered if I wanted to give that up. In addition to that, I was about to embark on another adventure, and did not want to worry about a new role while I was on vacation, so I tabled the thought, and took my vacation.

I was surprised to find that when I returned from my vacation, the position remained open, and that there was not a lot of internal interest in the role, which I thought was really strange. The Holidays rolled in, and many people took time off from work, which left me even more time to really think about my career directions. I knew I could do more, but was I willing to give up a job I loved, leadership I felt respected by, and a routine that I became the master of, to take a risk on something brand new. After a lot of consideration, discussions with several people whose opinion I valued highly, and my own soul searching, I decided to pursue the leadership role. I was the successful candidate, and as of March 1st, 2022, I assumed the Operations Manager role for my company's online programs.

During a lot of this time, my other passion was active as well, as it was time to start charting out potential adventure destinations. Just like the others, I started with a list of places that I still wanted to see, and what would be viable given accessibility, air fares, and current conditions. Throughout several of the stories in this book, I often mentioned of my desire to see the Holy Land area. It was the part of my 2020 trip to Egypt, that I had to cancel, because Israel did not open up the country for almost 2 years to foreign travelers. I was concerned about trying again, simply because Israel has been so stringent with entry, and the requirements after they allowed entry, that I felt it would be too much hassle to even enjoy the trip. Right around the middle of January 2022, the Israeli government started to change their stance on entry, and vaccine requirements started loosening, enough so, that I decided to see if I could finally make this long-awaited spiritual pilgrimage. Since I had planned this adventure out 2 years ago, the itinerary I wanted to do, and places I had wanted to see, were already mapped out. No new research was needed for me to set this trip up, which actually left me feeling quite bored for long periods running up to the trip, as it was all booked. I decided to pull the trigger at the end of January, and chose my dates for a late August departure, that would take me on a *"Holy Land Adventure"* to the countries of Israel, Palestine & Jordan. I was finally going to a land where so many stories I had heard as a youth took place. A place where 3 of the largest religions in the world lay claim to. A place where turmoil, fighting and religious wars have brewed for thousands of years. Whether you consider yourself a religious person, or just someone who has a love of history, there would be more than enough to satisfy one's travel palate, and it was now going to be my next great adventure.

The run up to departure date was really anti-climactic, in that there were no last-minute snags, or changes to bring a heightened level of stress. Most of the components for the trip had long been confirmed and paid for. Add to that the Covid fear had finally gone by the way side, so there wasn't anything for me to do, but wait out the days before departure day. Like always before, that day arrived, and soon I found myself on the way to the airport courtesy of my daughter Katie. Being it was a Sunday late morning, traffic was not a huge issue, but you never know traveling to LAX, so I wanted to get an early start to anticipate any unexpected issues.

When I travel internationally, I don't mind arriving considerably early for my flight, as I am able to enter the airline partner lounge, and wait out the time in considerable comfort and relaxation. As long as I am flying with an airline, or partner airline that I have frequent travel status with, I can usually make my way to the departure lounge. The extra time I had before the flight allowed me some time to think about how I would approach this particular adventure. Each trip I take has some unique characteristics, but this one was particularly different, because of the mixed emotions and religious connotations this destination would bring. I thought about how I wanted to craft the videos for the series to upload to my YouTube channel. Most of my videos are brought to life by use of music to fit the scenery, and did I want to follow that familiar path, or perhaps incorporate something a bit different. I did not have to decide a course right away, because I had many hours of flying to formulate my strategy, and see which direction appealed to me. With that in mind, it was time to head to the departure gate for what would be the first leg of this long trip to the Middle East.

London Calling

It is not an uncommon occurrence for me to squeeze in every ounce of time I have on my adventures, and if I can add that tiny bit extra into a trip, I will. Much like my other trips when I head over the Atlantic, I found a way to add some additional fun into this particular adventure. Staying true to my pattern of using foreign airlines for my adventures, I chose Virgin Atlantic, for this particular trip. I was able to build in an extended layover of 11 hours in one of my favorite cities, London. This was not my first-time visiting London; in fact, it was my 5th time visiting the Capital of the UK. I'll admit I have a special affinity for this city, as it was the first international city, I had ever visited back in 1986. However, 20 years have passed since I was last a guest of her Royal Majesty, and I felt it was time for a return visit, brief as it may be. Even though this was not my first time, there remained a couple of items that I had not seen in previous trips, and they were the must do's of this return trip.

One drawback about visiting a new place when traveling independently, is you are often unfamiliar with the normal routines and moving about. Fortunately, with London, none of that was an issue for me. I knew exactly which train and where to go when I got to *Heathrow Airport*, in order to head into the city. I bought my *London Travel Card*, which allowed me all day access on the London Underground transit system. I remembered the exact stations I needed to go to in order to see what I had on my mini agenda, and some of those stops included transfers to different underground lines.

In no time, I arrived at Victoria Station, which is one of the major stations in London that combines the underground system, and British Rail departures. This is also the closest station to the area that I wanted to start in. Victoria Station is in a prime area being close to Buckingham Palace, and was also close to the hotel I stayed at my very first time in London. As I walked along Buckingham Palace Road to the front of the palace entrance, it was not surprisingly fairly crowded with tourists, but pretty much remained the same as what I had remembered. A few photographs, and a video clip later, I headed down to the Westminster area, to see the Abbey, Houses of Parliament, and of course Big Ben, which recently had the renovation scaffolding removed. London weather is always an iffy proposition, and today was no different as the clouds were in and out, along with brief periods of sun. The contrast of the sky made for some great photos along the river Thames, with the government buildings as a back drop. A satisfying feeling to know that the traditions I had remembered were pretty much still intact, but it was time for something new.

While I truly enjoy doing the adventurous and obscure things when I travel, I am not at all adverse to doing the traditional and downright touristy things that others do either. Thus was the case when I hopped on the Jubilee Line (a new underground line for me), and headed for the St. John's Wood station, because I just had to walk across **Abbey Road Street.** I had not experienced this previously, and knew it was time to check this one off my list. Little more than a basic crosswalk of about maybe 35 feet, this area was filled with people simply walking across the street, much to the dismay of drivers actually traveling down the road. Drivers be damned, I was not giving up my 15 seconds of fame for anyone. Much the same as John, George and Ringo walked across, so too did Paul finally join them.

As the day grew late, I still had one more pop culture item I wanted to address, but this would require I get back on the Underground and head to Kings Cross Station, in the northern part of the city. For it is Kings Cross where the Hogwartz Express departs from to start every school year, and I just had to see the true **Platform 9¾**. The line to get your picture taken at the famous site was long and winding (Beatles), and I decided that seeing the actual spot would be enough, as I needed to head back to Heathrow for my continuing flight to Israel. Fortunately, the ride back was easy as I jumped on the Piccadilly Line, and rode all the way to Terminal 1 at the airport. My brief time in London was intense, but it was just the nostalgia I needed to reassure me that not everything changes. It would be the last time I would have the comfort of familiarity on this trip, as I was headed toward a whole set of "first times" and a host of unknowns.

A City Divided

Another overnight flight from London had me arriving in Tel Aviv at around 5:00am local time. Pretty much running on adrenaline only by this time, I made my way through immigration, and the intense scrutiny started. I was asked many question questions about where I was coming from, why was I traveling alone etc. My normal routine would have been to provide some sarcastic answer, but I quickly thought, this was not the time to be a smart ass, so I just answered the questions, and was granted access to the country. From here it was an easy train ride into the heart of Jerusalem, at a price that was a very reasonable 5.00 USD. Normally after a long flight I like to have a private car service from the airport, but in this case, prices ranged from $75.00 to $100.00 for a 20-minute ride, and I instead opted for a smooth train ride. This was my first real lesson in the expensive culture that is Israel.

Because I arrived so early into Jerusalem, and made my way to the hotel, my room was not yet ready, so I was unable to check in. I knew this was a possibility, but every once in a while, you catch a break, and they have a room to give you. I had about 4 hours before the room would be ready, and knew that if I even sat down for a couple of minutes, I could very easily fall asleep in the lobby. I left California on a Sunday afternoon, and after an overnight flight to London, running around for 10 hours there, and another 4-hour flight into Israel, I was running on fumes by Tuesday morning. I decided to walk around the old city, while waiting for my room, and discovered the 4 distinct areas of this 1.4 square kilometer area. There is a Muslim quarter, a Jewish quarter, a Christian quarter, and an Armenian quarter. Each of these areas have their own customs, and feelings about who really lays claim to this city as their capital. As such, the level of suspicion and lack of trust from one person to the next is palpable. The city of Jerusalem is by far the most disputed city in all of the world as 3 monotheistic religions claim it to be their capital. If there is one thing that everyone will agree upon about their religion, it's that theirs is always right. Still looking to kill time, I had a chance to visit the most disputed area in all of Jerusalem, The Temple Mount. This is an interesting area, in that the Temple is a Mosque, that non-Muslims may not enter, located on grounds that have several gates, but only one which non-Muslims can enter, except if you are Jewish, where you are requested not ascend to the Mount at all. Indeed, I found this was a very divided city. After my visit and quite a few photographs and a video clip, it was time to return to the hotel, and hoped I had a room ready. Success was had, as I checked into my room, and proceeded to immediately engage in a "nap" that lasted 17 hours into the next morning.

In His Footsteps

Having spent the better part of my first full day in Jerusalem catching up on much deserved rest, I started my 2nd day off early in the morning, and feeling quite energetic. That would be important because this was the day I had planned to learn about the birth & death of Jesus. Long before I arrived in Israel, I had decided that I would follow the Christian path for this adventure. Not because of a lack of interest in any other ideas, but to experience the stories that I was raised with upon growing up as a young protestant. During my travels, I have literally had an opportunity to witness almost every major religion that is widely known to man. Because of those experiences, I love understanding the core belief systems of each religion, and do so without any fear of conversion attempts, or brainwashing from those said religions. Since I was well versed in Christianity, I knew I would follow the stories of Jesus' life, and the experiences that historical accounts have provided us.

With that in mind, I found myself on bus 231 from the Damascus Gate bus station, on my way to the City of David, more commonly known as **Bethlehem**. Staying true to my form, and wanting to fit in, I decided to take the bus, as any other local probably would. Yes, I could have taken a taxi for the 10-kilometer ride, and paid a premium for the convenience, but wanted to just fit in. Now because Bethlehem is actually located in the **Palestinian Territory**, I needed to have my passport with me, because we would technically be crossing into another country. After about a 40-minute ride, I exited the bus at a small stop outside Bethlehem, and had about a 15-minute walk to the center of the town known as Manger Square. It was in this area where the Church of the Nativity is located. In addition to being the oldest active church in Israel, it is also the birth place of Jesus. The church has a very modest exterior, and was much more elaborate on the inside. A concept I would soon discover across most of the historical churches I would see. During my research, I had read that you should arrive at the church very early, as the crowds will arrive, and the long wait to see the birth sight of Jesus could be hours. With my arrival around 7:30am, I managed to avoid the crowds, but stumbled right into a full Latin Mass service right at the sight of Christ's birth. This mass lasted about 30 minutes, so I became well versed in a service, where I did not understand one word. I did however, have the opportunity to take communion, and they do not use grape juice, but the real thing. Closing out the mass service, I slipped back into my tourist mode, and had my picture taken while kneeling at the site of Jesus' birth, which was a very moving feeling.

The Church of the Nativity was the main draw for me in Bethlehem, but I still had plenty of time allocated for other things, so I managed to visit Shepherd's Field, and the famous olive wood factory, where all the custom crucifix crosses, and other Christian memorabilia are made. This is the same stuff that you will see in the malls during the holidays, and I was at ground zero for all of it. $300.00 later, I walked out the door, and headed toward the Separation Wall to see some of the Banksy artwork, along with art from lesser-known artists, and everyday people. The Separation Wall was erected by Israel as a boundary between Israel and The Palestinian Territory, with the stated goal of deterring terrorist activities. Much like the Berlin Wall was designed to keep the East Germans from fleeing, the Separation Wall is designed to keep the Palestinians from entering Israel. Entry for them is highly restricted, and heavily monitored by border patrol. Not to be outdone, Israeli citizens are forbidden to enter Bethlehem, so those Israelis who wish to see the birth place of the **King of the Jews** cannot. A rather sad and unfortunate situation all around, with no real solution on the horizon. Convinced that I could not solve the Middle East Peace Process, I had to return to Israel for the 2nd half of my day, as it was time to deal with the Death of Jesus.

Upon leaving Bethlehem at mid-day, I started to get the true sense of the desert climate of Israel. I was fully prepared to deal with the heat of the desert, but was completely caught off guard by how humid this arid climate was. I was no stranger to humidity with growing up in Pittsburgh, but for the last 35 years, I have resided in the dry climate of Southern California. The Holy Land seemed to provide both, as if it was a little "something for everyone". I caught the bus back from Palestine to the Old City, and even had some time to drop off my plethora of souvenirs that I purchased. There was no rest for the weary, as the second half of my day was all about the final days of Jesus, and the places of prominence surrounding that moment in time.

It started with me taking a quick bus ride up to the top of the **Mount of Olives**. While this route is walkable, the second thing I discovered about the Jerusalem area is that it is very hilly, think San Francisco. With the temperature hovering at around 92 degrees, and the humidity close to 90%, walking up the Mount, then walking back down, did not excite me. The bus let me off at the view point, and from there I was able to see the **Chapel of Ascension**. This is believed to be the place where Jesus ascended into Heaven, and is complete with a stone cast of the foot print of Jesus. From there, I started walking down the Mount, thru the largest Jewish cemetery in Israel, past the Church of Mary Magdalene, and into the **Garden of Gethsemane**, where Jesus was betrayed by Judas, and arrested by the Romans. Along the way, I met two young boys who started talking to me, and asking me questions. I made a brief video with them, as I always enjoy letting locals be a part of my vlog. They walked with me for a few minutes, until a guy in a car pulled about and started yelling at them in Hebrew. I later learned that they were professional pick pockets, specializing in stealing from tourists. A very good reminder, that regardless of how friendly the environment appears to be, you must always remain cautious.

Crossing into the Old City via the Lions Gate entrance, I found myself on the **Via Delarosa**. This is the street path that Jesus walked while carrying the cross on his back on the way to the site of his crucifixion. The path is highlighted with markers known as "stations", with each station having a significance of the journey. The final stations are within the Church of the Holy Sepulchre, which is the site of the crucifixion, and location of the cave where Jesus was buried, and his eventual resurrection, which Christians more commonly refer to as Easter. Spending time in this church was quite illuminating, and the history behind the whole story, culminating in this spot, was very surreal. While the focus of this day was on both the birth and death of Jesus, I still had a passion to understand what took place during those 33 years in between. A passion I hoped would be fulfilled the next day, as I booked an all-day tour to the region of Galilee.

The Miracles of Galilee

The day started early at 5:00am, as I walked to a central hotel for the pickup of my tour that would take me to the many towns along the **Sea of Galilee**. After about an 1:15 minute ride, we arrived in the town of Nazareth, where Jesus grew up. **Nazareth** is a town of about 75,000 residents, and the main drawing point is the **Church of Annunciation**. This is where the angel Gabriel appeared to the virgin Mary, and told her that should would be the mother of the savior. The church itself is a bit more modern on the outside, but inside, it was very ornate with lots of stained glass, and carved statues. Now it was time for the not so fun elements of escorted tours, the dreaded stop at the expensive souvenir shop, that they never tell you about. This has long been a pet peeve of mine, but they all seem to do it, and the hard sale begins. Fortunately, it lasted about 30 minutes and we were back on the bus heading to the next miracle site.

Cruising past the small town of Cana, where Jesus performed the "water into wine" miracle, it wasn't long before we stopped at the **Church of the Multiplication**. The site of this church is the location where Jesus fed 5000 listeners, with just 5 loaves of bread and 3 fishes. This was a relatively small church, with an original mosaic that dates back to the 5th century. Probably the most interesting thing here was after I filmed a video clip, a lady from the tour came over an asked if I was a pastor, and what church did I belong to. Not sure what led her to believe that I was a pastor, but politely told her that I wasn't, but filming for my YouTube channel. We still hadn't actually made it to the water, but that would change on our next stop, as we entered the town of **Capernaum**. Located right on the shore of the Sea of Galilee, this tiny town had a very tranquil feel as the waters were very calm, and it was quite peaceful, along with being 100 degrees, and humid. This day by far was the hottest I had experienced so far. It is written that in Capernaum, which by the way was the home of Peter, the first follower of Jesus, the miracle of walking on water, and the calming of the sea took place. After some time in this restful place, it was time to leave the Sea of Galilee, which is not really a sea, but is really a fresh water lake. It is the only fresh water lake in all of Israel. We still hard one more stop to make on this very long and hot day.

Given that the temperature was pushing 100 degrees, the concept of taking a dip in the river Jordan, would be a welcome addition to this day long tour. That is exactly where we ended up as the final stop for the day was at that Yardenit Baptismal site". This is an interesting place along the river, because it is very cleverly marketed as the Baptismal site, but not what most people will assume. This is "a" baptismal site, but not "the" baptismal site of Jesus, by John. That actual location is about an hour and a half South of this location along the Israel/Jordan border. This location is touted as a baptismal site because people can, and do, get baptized in this area of the Jordan river. This location was opened back in 1981, because the original location of Jesus' baptism is an area now more militarized, so this area was opened to allow people to come and partake in the baptism experience. Either way, I was going to have my experience in the Jordan river, and not get hung up on the specifics of which location is officially accurate. Wading in the river, was again just another opportunity for me to "walk through history" the way hundreds of thousands of religions pilgrims do on a yearly basis. Certainly, this day long tour provided me a greater understanding of the religious teachings and stories I grew up with, but also an opportunity to cool off on what was the hottest day of the entire trip. A late afternoon arrival back in Jerusalem had me exhausted and ready for an adventure break. Since the next day was a down day, with no real agenda, I took the opportunity to perhaps revisit a few places that I may have rushed through the first time, such as the **Western Wall**, and the Church of the Holy Sepulchre. I knew I had to take advantage of this time, because the rest of the trip was scheduled to be jam packed.

Secular Saturday

With my first 3 days in Israel almost exclusively devoted to the religious aspects of the area, I was ready for a more tourist driven experience, yet continue to retain my trademark of adventure travel. So, my focus shifted to the Negev desert, where I would visit two very famous spots within Israel, but still maintain my untraditional flair for experiences. A 3:00 am departure South would bring me to my first stop, the Fortress of Masada. This fortress was a palace built by King Herod in the year 31BC, where it served as his "escape from the world" home. Many years later it became prominent again when a group of Israelis frustrated with Roman rule, assumed control of the area, until the Romans finally gained control in 76 AD. The majority of people who visit Masada will ascent to the top of the mountain via the cable car that was built. In less than 10 minutes you can be at the top, and seeing the ruins of the once mighty fortress.

However, for the more adventurous, one can also hike to the top via a trail known as the "snake path". Many people will do this in the early morning hours in order to be at the top to catch the sunrise. The cable car service doesn't begin until around 8:00am, and thus you will have missed the sunrise. This method of ascending Masada had all the ear markings of a Paul "must do", and so at 5:15am on this already hot day in the desert, I along with maybe 20 other people started our ascent to the top. The reviews of the snake path vari in terms of difficulty, and as I discovered in South Africa the year before, the term "easy" is relative to each individual. As I continued to climb, it became more and more difficult as the grade, and the sheer number of steps associated with this hike, seemed to grow and grow. There were a couple of points during this time where I asked myself if what I had accomplished was enough, and was the will to push on really worth it. Refusing to give up, I finally crawled into the cable car station, where the rest of the walk was flat. I had made it to the top, with a shirt completely covered in sweat as the temperature at 6:20am, was a cool 95 degrees. Please spare me with "it's a dry heat", hot is hot is hot. After all that work, I was greeted with a low hanging fog that really impeded much of the sunrise anyway. Filming a few clips, and walking around the grounds for about 20 minutes, it was time for me to descend. I had done what I had set out to do, but discovered the ends don't always justify the means. Not to worry, as we had two more stops to make on this desert part of the adventure.

Feeling pretty tired, and extremely hot from the early morning hike, I made my way back to the air-conditioned bus enroute to our next stop of the day, which would be the nature reserve of **Ein Gedi**. This is another hiking area in the desert, however, one that is flush with waterfalls with which to cool off in, so it would be a welcome respite, even for the briefest of moments. I had my doubts about this stop, as it is often the stop that most tourist reviews feel is pretty much a waste of time. The stop was for only 2 hours, so you can't really do much hiking in that time, but I made my way to the first waterfall area, and decided I had enough hiking for the day, and just relaxed in the cool waters, and sounds of the crashing falls. After the extreme heat of Masada, I was grateful for the opportunity to just rest in a much cooler environment. This was really the prelude to the last stop, which is what most of the people on the tour were anxious for, and that was the opportunity to experience the lowest place on planet Earth, The Dead Sea.

The Dead Sea like the Sea of Galilee is not a sea at all, but a lake. This lake however sits at 420 meters below sea level, which makes is the lowest spot in the entire world. I had a flash back to 5 years ago, when I stood before the highest place in the world at Mt. Everest, and now, I was at the complete opposite of that. The Dead Sea derives its name because it is a lake that has no life contained within it at all. The salt content of this lake measures in at 30% which makes it impossible to host any type of life. To better illustrate the magnitude of the salt level, the salinization level of the Atlantic or Pacific Ocean is around 3%. A by-product of this high salt content is that a person cannot sink in the water, but will float without the assistance of any swimming maneuvers. Floating is what everyone comes to the Dead Sea to do, along with rubbing the mineral rich mud on your body to help purify the skin. Another by-product of that high salt content which is not so pleasant is that any cuts or recent changes to the skin, can cause burning sensations. I soon realized that the Dead Sea would not be kind to the fact that I had shaved in the early morning, and that the areas of my neck and chin would soon realize that burning.

The novelty of floating and covering my body with layers of mud soon wore off after about 30 minutes, so I decided to use one of the available showers to rinse myself free of salt and mud, then changed back into my clothes, that still retained the smell of sweat. With about an hour of free time left before we would head back to Jerusalem, I decided to seek out something much more to my liking as I discovered the Lowest Bar in the World. Here I tried a local Israeli lager, and just enjoyed the cool misters that were spraying the fine water as a means of outdoor air conditioning. Not long after I finished my beer, we were headed back to our starting point in Jerusalem, where it was still midafternoon, and a chance to rest, before embarking out for my last night in the old city.

Crossing Jordan

These 3:00am departure pickups were becoming a bit silly, but that's what I found myself doing again this fine Sunday morning, as I was off to the **Hashemite Kingdom of Jordan**. It started with a 4-hour drive to the border town of Eilat near the Red Sea (Which actually is a sea). It would be here that we would cross into Jordan, and continue for the next 3 days in yet another new country for me. Because of the political climate of relations, the Israeli guide would leave us, and once we crossed the border, we would be received by a Jordanian guide. When we entered into Jordan, I noticed the people were very friendly from the beginning, and that a lot of the tense feelings found within Jerusalem seemed to disappear. The entry was fairly smooth, and soon we were on our bus with our guide **Nizar Ali**, on our way to the port city of Aqaba.

Our final destination for the day would be a Bedouin camp in the Wadi Rum desert, but first there was time to take a seaside break in Aqaba. We stopped at a local resort, that allowed us to rest, and enjoy the Red Sea. After about 3 hours at the beach club, we headed into the desert to our home for the night, which would be a tented Bedouin camp in the area known as Wadi Rum. One of the highlights of this area is the amazing red sand desert, and the incredible rock formations that surround this entire area. All of this was captured with a majestic Jeep safari ride that took us out to sand dunes, and an alluring sandstone arch formation to watch the sunset. In all of my travels around the world, I have seen white sand, black sand and even pink sand, but this was my first time experiencing red sand.

When we arrived at the Arch, Nizar motioned to me to head to the middle of the arch in order to take a picture of me. Little did he know of my intense fear of heights, and as he snapped a few photos, I managed to hold it together without him being any the wiser. One of his pictures turned out to be one of my top 5 photos of the entire trip. As the sun dropped below the rocks, it was time to head back to the camp and prepare for the traditional Bedouin dinner that awaited us. It was the most food I had eaten the entire trip, all in the setting of a night sky littered with a million stars. The dinner was followed by a Bedouin show that soon had me closing my eyes as another very long day was in the books. It was important to get a good night's rest, as the next day would be the pinnacle of this trip, and the chance to chalk up another Wonder of the World.

The Red Rose City

The morning started with a bit of a "sleep in" till 6:30am. While most of the time I would not consider that a "sleep in", my risings on this trip were such that it provided a good 3 hours more than normal. I did not mind the early rise, as this was the day I had been looking forward to for quite some time, because we would be heading to **Petra**. Often referred to as the Red Rose City, Petra was believed to have been founded as far back as the 4th century BC, by a group of Nomadic tribes known as the **Nabataens**. This city thrived for hundreds of years along an area that was part of the **Silk Road**. Like many places during these early times, Petra fell victim to the Romans around the year 103AD, and with the rise of Islam, became relatively hidden from the world around the 360AD period. It remained virtually hidden until the year 1812 when it was re-discovered by a Swiss traveler. Over the years, Petra has become Jordan's most iconic tourist destination, boosted largely because of the UNESCO's designation of 7 New Wonders of the World, along with prominent roles in movies, most notably, **Indiana Jones and the Last Crusade**. If ever there was a place for me to have a new adventure, this was the place.

We left the Bedouin camp around 8:00am for what would be about a 2-hour ride to the town of **Wadi Musa**, where Petra is located. As we started the journey, Nizar shared with us his assessment of the historical situation of this volatile area known as the Middle East. Nizar, who is Jordanian by birth, but lived in America for many years, had a very unique perspective, and drew an unparalleled analogy using technology that I had ever heard. His reasoning was sound and logical, and while I may not have agreed with all of his conclusions, he certainly left me with a perspective I had not thought about previously. That my friends, is why I travel and meet other people. To walk away with a new perspective, or to at least think that maybe I am not always right. A concept that all three of the major religions of this area, do not take into account.

About 30 minutes outside of our arrival, we stopped a local rest stop for some coffee, restroom etc. The location was atop a mountain where below in the distance you could see Petra. This rest stop unfortunately was probably one of the disappointments of the trip, as we became subjected to a lot of high-pressure souvenir salespeople, using a charity associated to Queen Noir as justification for spending on overpriced souvenirs. The situation became somewhat uncomfortable for me and some other people, that we made our way back to the bus, and waited in the heat for the tour to commence. We were close now, so I wasn't going to let this little issue detract from the day.

We arrived at the Petra Visitor Center, and Nizar secured the entry tickets for the group. From here, he warned us to be prepared for a lot of walking, and I would soon find out exactly what he meant. We started hiking towards the area known as the Siq "Seek". This is a rock canyon that goes for about 1.2 kilometers before it opens to one of the most famous structures in the world, **The Treasury,** or in Arabic (Al Khazneh). This façade is cut out of the rock and is by far one of the most well-known landmarks in the world, and it was now checked off my bucket list. After numerous pictures from a variety of angles, we continued further into the Lost City to see other landmarks. I wanted to take my time, because I had a second full day in the city tomorrow, so I didn't feel the need to rush. After checking out the **Streets of Facades**, the amphitheater, and many other cave areas, I started to head back to the main entrance. I would be returning later tonight to witness **"Petra by Night"**, so I wanted to get a little rest, and a chance to clean up as this was another very warm day.

Petra by Night is an opportunity to re-enter the city in the evening, with the Siq, and the main square of the Treasury lit up with hundreds of candles. It is only offered 3 evenings a week, and I had planned my trip to be there during one of those 3 nights. Essentially, all of the walking I did earlier in the day, would need to be repeated. This was something I soon found out had serious consequences that would dog me for the rest of my trip. I decided to walk from my hotel back to the Visitor Center, which was almost 2 miles. Then proceeded to walk back into Petra, in the dark, through the Siq, and on to the Treasury. The show lasted about 30 minutes or so, and then I walked back out. My left foot started a feel a bit uncomfortable during the walk in, and only got worse on the way back out. It became so bad that I had to take a taxi from the Visitor Center back to the hotel, as I was unable to walk anymore. When I got back to the hotel, and took off my hiking boots, I found what would be the makings of a blister on my instep. I soaked my feet in some warm water just to help relax them, and then headed off to sleep, hoping that a decent rest would help.

When I woke the next morning, I discovered a huge blister had developed that was about the size of a quarter, and I could not place any weight on that foot. My plan for the day was to hike even further to another area of the city to see the famous Monastery, which was about an hour further out from the Treasury. I was able to drain the blister, and wrap it with some bandages, but could put very little weight on it. The Monastery was not going to happen for sure, but would I even be able to do anything else. After a very good tape job, I got myself into a position where I could walk again, and so I decided to at least go back to the Treasury, and see that area again before I left. I took things very slow, and walked more cautiously, and made it back into the main area for one last glimpse of the amazing Red Rose City. By late afternoon, we were on our way back to the border crossing near Aqaba for our return into Israel. The Jordanian border guards were very friendly, and thanked me for visiting their country. This was a far cry from my arrival on the Israeli side, where they proceeded to ask me if I was carrying any bombs, guns or other weapons. One particularly annoying question to me again was "why was I traveling alone". Was this a better time to perhaps be a "smart ass"? I chose to just smile and answer politely.

Tel Aviv

The drive back from the border to Tel Aviv would take about 4 hours, meaning this was just another in a long line of 16–18-hour days I would experience on this trip. Since Tel Aviv was my starting and ending point for the trip, it seemed logical to take a couple of days to experience the commercial side of Israel, without all of the religious elements as a back drop. This would also be a situation where I had nothing structurally planned, just 2 days to relax and do whatever moved me. One thing that Israel is well known for is a very large hostel accommodation presence. The hostel crowd tends to be young and traveling on a budget, and is also popular with people hiking through for a short stay. I had never done this in my younger days, as the shared bathroom arrangement is pretty much a deal breaker for me. There have been a few instances where I have endured a shared bathroom, but usually for just 1 night. Base Camp at Mt. Everest is one example of that. One chain of hostels in Israel that has a good reputation is **Abraham Hostels**, and since they offer accommodations with a private bathroom, I decided to give them a try for a 2-night stay. The room I got was very basic, but did have a private bathroom, and included breakfast for $132.00 per night, inexpensive by Israel standards.

I spent the better part of 2 days just walking around Tel Aviv, albeit rather gingerly since I still had a sore foot. I spent a lot of time down at the beach promenade just enjoying the Mediterranean Sea, enjoying some fish and chips, and the occasional beer, all the while feeling the calming effect of the sea sounds. It felt good to just relax, and not feel controlled by a set schedule. I always try to cram as much adventure into these trips as I can, and often feel the effects of that decision when I return home. This was one instance where I took some time to power down before returning home. I had a chance to absorb all that I had seen the previous 10 days, and analyze what really moved me, and what I had learned. I took time to experience the local markets, and make use of the local transportation options, and soon it was time for me to head out to the airport for my late evening flight back to America. The train ride, check in process, and the flight home were as seamless as one could hope for when traveling internationally in this day & age.

My Takeaways

The Holy Land Adventure was by far my most ambitious and physically demanding trip to date. Most every day was filled with something to do that challenged my stamina and physical fitness, whether it was climbing, walking, or just enduring long days in intense heat and humidity. I have been asked if this was a life changing trip for me by many people. All of my trips are life changing in some way or another, but I think because of the religious elements at play, many people feel that some form of transformation takes place. I didn't return from the Holy Land with a white beard, or the ability to walk on water. I will share my answer that I told all of the people who asked me that perplexing question. A trip to the Holy Land is a trip of faith. One must believe that what you are seeing, is exactly what is described. Did I kneel before the birth place of Christ? Did I stand on the spot where Jesus fed 5000 people with enough food that normally would have fed a couple of people? Did I stand at the spot where Jesus was crucified? The stories tell me I did, and therefore my faith tells me I did as well. The Holy Land is well worth the trip if you are looking for spiritual validation, or even if you are only looking for just another walk, through history.

Dome of the Rock at the Temple Mount
(Jerusalem, Aug 2022)

Birth Place of Jesus Christ
(Bethlehem, Aug 2022)

Banksy Art Work
(Palestine, Aug 2022)

View of Jerusalem from the Mount of Olives
(Jerusalem, Aug 2022)

Baptismal Site on the River Jordan
(Yardenit, Sept 2022)

Overlooking the Dead Sea
(Dead Sea, Sept 2022)

Arch in Wadi Rum Desert
(Wadi Rum, Sept 2022)

The Treasury el Khazneh
(Petra Jordan, Sept 2022)

With my guide, Nizar
Ali in Petra
(Petra Jordan, Sept 2022)

14.

My Way

Throughout the many pages of this book, I have managed to sprinkle in as many music metaphors as I could possibly think of. But if there is one music reference that sums up this entire book, or perhaps even my life for the last 10 years, it would be the title of this chapter. I have for the better part of my adult life, thrived on the concept of someone telling me I can't do something, only to turn around and do that very thing. I have often said that the worst 4 letter word I can think of is "can't". Over the last several years we have had a series of elected officials, and opportunistic so called "specialists" telling us what we can and can't do, all under the guise of public health and safety. Sadly, the majority of people allowed that to run their lives, at the expense of their social and physical health. As I write this chapter, I heard a news story today that Howard Stern had just recently left his home for the first time since the start of the pandemic. How sad is that when the person most known at one time as the maverick who would thumb his nose at anyone who disapproved of his thoughts and opinions, has become such a germaphobe, who is afraid to interact with others because of Covid.

Why my defiant stance on this issue you ask? We have one life to live, and because we often focus on the quantity of that life, rather than the quality, our priorities become misplaced. Each of us has the opportunity to live out our lives pretty much in a manner that we choose. However, there are many people who I have met traveling the world that do not enjoy that privilege, as I have seen first-hand. For over 2+ years, I heard nothing but directives that we could not travel, we had to stay home, we could not be social, all built on a premise of fear. I did all of these things and more, and managed to learn a few things along the way. I traveled to places where the popular narrative is that it is dangerous, or the population does not like Americans, or that governments of said places are bad, and we should consider them an enemy. I think the hard truth to accept is that the people who dislike Americans the most, are other Americans! That is the importance of being fortunate enough to have my feet on the ground in other countries, and to actually experience the culture in real time. International relations just like a virus can be predicated on fear, and distort the truth for the benefit of others. It's up to each of us to seek the truth for ourselves, and not allow somehow to provide you with their truth.

I have found the way to my truth is through travel & adventure, for you, it may be some other mechanism. I don't expect everyone to agree with every premise I have written in this book, but if you at least allow yourself to step outside the notion that I'm right, you're wrong, and be open to the concept that there may be another idea, you may see the world in a different light. Each of us has our own dream, and mine just happens to be traveling the world. Whatever your dream is, wouldn't you just love to experience it on your terms, and be proud, the way I am to say that "I did it my way"?